THERE ARE NO TRIVIAL MOMENTS.

CLIF SMITH

MIND FUL NESS

WITHOUT THE BELLS AND BEADS

Unlocking Exceptional Performance,
Leadership, and Well-Being for
WORKING PROFESSIONALS

WILEY

Published by John Wiley & Sons, Inc., Hoboken, New Jersey.
Published simultaneously in Canada.

For general information on our other products and services or for technical support, please contact our Customer Care Department within the United States at (800) 762-2974, outside the United States at (317) 572-3993 or fax (317) 572-4002.

Wiley publishes in a variety of print and electronic formats and by print-on-demand. Some material included with standard print versions of this book may not be included in e-books or in print-on-demand. If this book refers to media such as a CD or DVD that is not included in the version you purchased, you may download this material at http://booksupport.wiley .com. For more information about Wiley products, visit www.wiley.com.

Mention of specific companies, organizations, or authorities in this book does not imply endorsement by the author or publisher, nor does mention of specific companies, organizations, or authorities imply that they endorse this book, its author, or the publisher.

The recommendations made in this book are not meant to replace formal medical or psychiatric treatment. Individuals with medical or psychological problems should consult with their physician or therapist about following the program in this book.

Mindfulness meditation has been around for thousands of years and has been written and spoken about by tens of thousands of people. It is easy to inadvertently write something that is similar to what someone else wrote without knowing it and therefore not giving them credit. In writing this book, I've tried to give credit where credit is due and hope any inadvertent turn of a phrase that matches someone else's without the proper acknowledgment is seen as an honest mistake rather than a deliberate attempt to copy or plagiarize.

Library of Congress Cataloging-in-Publication Data is Available:

ISBN 9781119750765 (Hardcover)
ISBN 9781119750833 (ePDF)
ISBN 9781119750826 (ePub)

Cover Design: Wiley
Cover Image: © Sergey Pakulin/Getty Images

SKY10025351_030521

To my mother, Vicki, for being like the sun. You have always given me warmth, light, and love without expecting anything in return.

To my son, Alexander, for reminding me I had eyes like a child once, too, and for helping me find them again.

To my wife, Jennifer, for your love and unwavering support on our journey together.

Contents

Foreword

TAL GOLDHAMER

We first met just before Clif was to speak with 4,000 of EY's newly promoted managers at the firm's annual Milestones event. Having heard great things about Clif's impact on so many people, it was a highly anticipated meeting for me.

Clif's towering height quickly gives way to his authentic words and genuine care for fellow humans. This first meeting centered on Clif's decision on whether to shift his career and life, yet again, and follow his heart and passion to bring mindfulness to even more people. Clif wanted to make a dent in the world by helping people live happier, healthier, and more productive lives. A heavy conversation before a big keynote. For most, it might throw them off. For Clif, it was an opportunity to personally practice mindfulness. Shortly after finishing our chat, Clif hit the stage and masterfully captured the crowd.

Despite being unknown to the audience and delivering his keynote wedged between an acclaimed Harvard professor and a *New York Times* bestselling author, Clif's talk was rated the highest. It is a testament to the power of his story, combined with an ability to be vulnerable and connect with an audience, that he can successfully introduce mindfulness to skeptics. We continue to work closely since that day.

Too often, mindfulness gets mistakenly characterized as a wellness concept that belongs outside the scope of a learning organization, which is otherwise focused on developing highly skilled leaders and technically competent professionals. Clif's approach of framing mindfulness as a way to impact performance, leadership, *and* well-being is unique, and his results are compelling.

In just a few years, Clif has reached over 60,000 people with his keynotes, workshops, and courses . . . with consistently exceptional feedback. The measured business and personal impact of the programs are similarly impressive, as covered later in this book.

When we evaluated moving mindfulness into our formal curriculum and developing a plan to scale it to even more people, it was a no brainer. It's been a great decision and a wonderful partnership.

Clif's impact continues to spread throughout our firm and also with clients. They have called on Clif and his team to introduce mindfulness to their leaders and people at all levels and help them establish effective mindfulness programs.

It's exciting that Clif has put his powerful story in writing and combined it with a practical, authentic, and no-nonsense guide to developing a consistent mindfulness practice.

Wishing you the same level of impact that our people at EY have received from Clif's approach to mindfulness and life.

Tal Goldhamer, Partner and Americas Chief Learning Officer,
Ernst & Young LLP

Introduction

A STAGGERED START

Most people will never become nor even try to become a US Army Chinese linguist, a CIA-trained case officer, a diplomat, or a Harvard graduate. These types of achievements, it's commonly believed, are reserved for exceptionally gifted individuals, the privileged old-monied elite, or private school–trained children of well-connected corporate or political power couples. It begs the question, then, how someone born into a poor family, living in a trailer with no college-educated family members, could ever become any one of those things, let alone all four and more? Many people think being born into a situation like that is tantamount to a life sentence of destitution and poverty. They would be wrong; there are repeatable paths from poverty to prosperity, but you only see them if you pay close attention and you only take those paths if you can get out of your own way.

I was kind of a late bloomer. You know the type: tall skinny kid in high school who lacks the kind of coordination needed to play any sport that requires complex physical activity or strength. I could, however, generally run in a straight line given enough motivation. The first time I thought about participating in sports, in a meaningful way, was when I decided to try out for the track team in 11th grade because my girlfriend was on the team. (Yay, motivation!) All I knew about track and field was what I vaguely remembered seeing on TV during the 1988 summer Olympics and, for some reason, the decathlon sticks out as my only memory as I write these words in 2020.

As you can imagine, I knew next to nothing about running track. When I finally joined the team, I was surprised that the runners' starting positions were staggered. In the starting position immediately before a race begins, the runner on the inside lane (lane 1) is at the primary starting line, and the runner in the outermost lane (lane 8) is positioned far ahead, 53.02 meters ahead to be exact.[1] The runners in lanes 2 through 7 were incrementally further "ahead" of the runner in lane 1, with the runner in lane 8 being the furthest "ahead."

This baffled me (I never took geometry in high school) and upset me because the coach assigned me to lane 1 for my first training race before I understood why starting lanes were designed this way. As I approached the starting line, I complained under my breath that everyone else was starting ahead of me. Once the gun went off it was my thoughts doing the racing. I thought, over and over again, about how unfair it all was to be put at such a disadvantage and there was no way I could ever catch up to the guy in lane 8 given such a fortunate advantage. Needless to say, I bombed the race and finished dead last. This same scene played out during my first couple practices.

What you probably knew in middle school, and what I eventually figured out in 11th grade, is that the distance around the track from the staggered starting spots to the finish line are actually the same for each lane. The "disadvantage" for the runner in lane 1 and the "advantage" for the runner in lane 8 were only in my mind. They were illusions. They were a result of my misperception of reality. After a few races I began to realize the runner in lane 8 was always way out in front at the start of the race but as it began and progressed, the entire field of runners generally came to be running nearly together as they closed in on the finish line. Once I gained a more accurate perception of reality, those unhelpful thoughts began to gradually subside and I began to place higher in the races.

I had been experiencing the exact opposite of the placebo effect. The placebo effect is that fascinating wonder of the human mind wherein individuals are given fake medicine, aka "a placebo," but nonetheless realize measurable improvements in a health condition due to their own expectation that the "medicine" is helping them. The placebo effect is so powerful that the US Food and Drug Administration uses it as a key factor in their evaluation criteria when considering a drug for approval, and doctors will even sometimes give patients a placebo instead of a drug with an active ingredient.[2] That's how powerful our thoughts, beliefs, and expectations can be.

So, in just the same way but with the opposite impact, my internal thoughts, beliefs, and expectations about other runners' advantages and about my disadvantages negatively influenced my performance in each race. Furthermore, the unhelpful thoughts and the negative effects didn't immediately stop after learning about the equal distances regardless of track lane placement. There was a lingering effect despite knowing the "truth" of the matter. This had a powerful impact on the level of importance I placed on understanding what

I was doing with my own mind and how it affected me. The key lessons I learned were that what you do with your mind matters, and even when you have an epiphany or insight about the "truth" of some situation or circumstance, it still takes diligent effort and a focused mind to continue to prevent yourself from falling into the same trap over and over again.

I felt like I had discovered a superpower but didn't really know how to use it. Fortunately, I had already received some initial mindfulness training to become more aware of the tendencies of the mind, but it took me a little while to begin practicing those skills in earnest and see my small investments in time and effort grow into a totally different conversation with life.

The "staggered start" analogy is really a metaphor for life in a number of ways. In this life, we tend to notice others who have it better than we do (folks with advantages) much more often than we notice people who have it worse (folks with disadvantages). We compare ourselves "up" versus comparing ourselves "down." Therefore, many of us are in a constant state of feeling we would be just as successful as those people with the advantages if only we had the same advantages. Unfortunately, this isn't the only way our brains distort reality.

When comparing ourselves to others with many advantages—and there are real advantages out there—we also tend to unconsciously overlook any disadvantages inherent in others' circumstances. For example, we might be able to imagine many advantages enjoyed by the children of a CEO of a Fortune 500 company and a successful business-owning spouse. Children of parents like that probably go to the best private schools, attend amazing summer camps where they continue learning and growing, and have allowances that would make the average wage earner salivate. They probably take enriching overseas trips and ski at the best resorts when they go on vacation. Of course, they also have their college tuition and expenses covered and maybe even get accepted into an Ivy League school because their father or mother attended and made a big donation. These are real advantages. Are there any drawbacks?

Children of the wealthy do not have to experience money problems. It's unlikely they've had their electricity or water turned off due to nonpayment. They've probably not had to decide which of their things they should pack as they prepare to move to a new apartment due to rent increases or job layoffs and they can't take everything because the new, cheaper place is much smaller. They may have never experienced the need to wear their older sibling's clothes so the family could save money. Resilience and grit are born out of facing and overcoming such obstacles and challenges, not by never facing them. These qualities are a big advantage for those who possess them and a big disadvantage for those who don't.

CEOs and business owners often work insane hours to rake in their high six- and seven-figure salaries and may only see their children a couple hours a day on the weekends. Is that an advantage for the children? Children's easy access to money with less supervision often confers easier access to unhealthy things such as drugs and alcohol. Can you think of any wealthy families' children who've gotten themselves into trouble or worse because of addiction? According to a study from 2017, kids in wealthier communities are using drugs and alcohol and drinking to intoxication at rates two to three times the national averages for their age groups.[3] Is that an advantage?

Comparing yourself to people who have more success and wealth than you do and attributing it solely to them being given a better lot in life is like me thinking the runner in lane 8 has an advantage. They do if you look at their circumstances with a very narrow and one-sided perspective. I easily saw and fixated on how far out in front the runner in lane 8 was but failed to see that by being in lane 1, my distance around the first turn was much shorter. I saw all his advantages and none of mine while seeing none of his disadvantages and all of mine. Seeing in this way is a trick of the mind in order to protect a fragile ego. It's an illusion. It's very difficult to accept that it's our decisions that matter most in our successes and failures in life, much more so than the circumstances into which we were born. What you focus on and the stories you tell yourself have an outsized impact on the quality of your life. This is where mindfulness comes in handy.

. . .

For far too long, mindfulness in the West has been nearly exclusively associated with spirituality and/or wellness. People seeking enlightenment or relief from stress, anxiety, and pain have been the primary audience. Therefore, most mindfulness teachers have continued to discuss mindfulness within that frame. That frame has been so narrow for so long it might seem that mindfulness is only for the spiritually inclined, or for people with challenging medical issues, such as panic attacks, paralyzing anxiety, and deep depression, or people who just want some stress relief. That couldn't be further from the truth.

I believe mindfulness today is where executive coaching was 20 to 30 years ago. Back then, no self-respecting managers or executive leaders would admit they had an executive coach. The fear that kept them quiet was that it might make it look like they *needed* a coach. Back then coaching was (thought to be) only for ne'er-do-wells who couldn't hack it on their own and needed a helping hand. The framing that executive coaching could help you go from good to great had not been constructed yet, even though, most nights on television, we could see hundreds of elite professional athletes such as Michael Jordan, Larry Bird, Joe Montana, Jerome Bettis, Monica Seles, Gabriela Sabatini, and so many others at the top of their games still getting coached. Eventually, the corporate world caught on and now almost all executive leaders have had some form of coaching to help them up their game.

Mindfulness is on the cusp of finally making that leap out of the frame that you only do it if you feel you are "broken" and can't handle the rough-and-tumble modern world or when the wheels are coming off your life and you're having an existential crisis. Having an "underlying condition" is not required to benefit from mindfulness. It can help you go from good to great when it comes to your performance, leadership, *and* well-being. Keeping mindfulness framed only in spirituality and wellness/stress relief limits its reach and impact.

Fortunately, there are some who have started to see this potential. Many in the sports world have dropped the term "mindfulness" and just call it "mental conditioning," which has enabled it to spread widely across professional athletes. Some companies have seen mindfulness's potential for leadership and performance enhancement and have begun to implement programs. The Mindful Leadership program, which we started in 2015 at Ernst & Young (EY), one of the Big Four firms, has affected more than 60,000 of our people through their attendance at my Mindful Leadership in the Modern World keynote, our 8-week Mindful Leadership at EY course, or one of our other mindfulness training and practice sessions. In just five short years, we went from teaching to six people around a dusty conference room table to presenting mindfulness to our most senior executive leaders around the boardroom table.

Unfortunately, not all of the corporate programs are as successful as EYs. We began to frame mindfulness as an avenue to exceptional leadership early on and were extremely diligent about keeping the teaching secular. However, that doesn't seem to be happening across the board and it's a detriment to the impact mindfulness can have. Of those few teachers and organizations who have attempted to step out of the binary frame of the spiritual- or wellness-focused approach, many tend to continue to bring in spiritual accessories regardless of their audience.

Attending my first mindfulness teacher training course was quite a shock. In the morning on the first day, the teachers came into the room holding small bells, wearing Buddhist beads, and carrying special cushions on which they meditated. This struck me as odd, because I had signed up for the "secular" mindfulness teacher training. It did not take long to gather that this "secular" training was going to be deeply intertwined with overtly spiritual and new-age thoughts, positions, and perspectives. There were—I kid you not—even Tarot card readings at an evening event and scores of participant comments during the training were met with the response, "That's so beautiful." If you want to turn off a corporate audience and never be invited back beyond what your original contract stipulated, just do what's in this paragraph.

I have no problem with those things in and of themselves; people can do what they want. I have read dozens of books and ancient writings on spirituality, Hinduism, Buddhism, Christianity, and so on, as well as traveled to Dharamshala, India, and meditated mere feet away from His Holiness, the Dalai Lama, but in the context of a training program being billed as secular, it was extremely off-putting. I quickly realized if these teachers were to show up at my company to try to teach mindfulness, they would be bringing with them nearly every stereotype people often associate with mindfulness and mindfulness teachers. In the corporate world, where there is no place for religious, spiritual, or new-age proselytizing, this could be devastating, because it only takes one "secular" mindfulness teacher describing their "invisible connection to the divine energy of the universe" to get a corporate mindfulness program canceled.

The fact that so many mindfulness teachers and advocates seem incapable of separating bells, beads, and spiritual beliefs (and, increasingly, political beliefs) from how they teach and describe mindfulness is a huge problem, because it alienates millions of people who could actually benefit from the practice. Additionally, many people who put shingles out as mindfulness "teachers" have rose-colored views of what mindfulness can do. They erroneously think, and are purveyors of the myth, that mindfulness is a path to only having joyous thoughts, being blissed out, seeing rainbows and butterflies everywhere, and being happy all the time.

I don't know why you picked up this book, but given the title it might be that you've had the thought, "What the hell is all the hype about mindfulness?" You may be one of the millions of people who have been curious about mindfulness but don't want to be associated with the spiritual crowd that so often drowns out its core meaning. Perhaps you recoil at the thought of listening to someone breathlessly guide meditations in a sickly sweet voice. Maybe you thought you'd need to join a yoga studio and get a subscription for monthly deliveries of incense. If any of those have been keeping you from trying out mindfulness, this book is for you. In these pages, I peel back the layers of hype and hyperbole about mindfulness and provide a practical and demystified approach to reaping the real benefits from a consistent mindfulness practice over just an 8-week period.

When I was approached by Wiley Publishing about writing a book, I knew my purpose would be the same as my purpose for delivering my keynotes, coaching high-performers, and teaching my 8-week mindfulness course: to creatively inspire others so that they may transcend self-limiting beliefs, achieve their dreams, and navigate life with a bit more ease.

As you progress through the book and do the exercises, you can gain a greater ability to respond thoughtfully and calmly in the midst of high-pressure and complex situations, become more agile in the face of change, and pay more attention to the things you deem most important. You will learn practices that are known to lead to enhanced mental focus, empathy, and resilience. Through consistent practice, you can become aware of some of your self-created challenges and learn ways to avoid automatically falling into the same patterns so you can get out of your own way. You will learn ways to be less affected by unhelpful internal dialogue, limiting beliefs, and irrational feelings of fear (failure, embarrassment, and criticism), allowing you to see and seize opportunities to grow beyond what you previously thought possible and unlock your latent potential. Finally, you'll also begin to be able to connect with people around you more fully and effectively. These benefits cascade and compound, resulting in improvements in performance, leadership, and well-being.

The book is divided into two primary parts. Part I, beginning with my story and how mindfulness has affected my life, is designed to demystify and define mindfulness (the *what*), discuss the science and benefits of mindfulness practice in the modern world (the *why*), and provide you with some initial exercises to begin increasing your base level of mindfulness (the very basic *how*). These are the fundamentals. I won't be going into a deep scholarly review of ancient texts and parsing the different definitions asserted by Pali and Sanskrit language experts. My goal here is to provide practical, useful, and non–new age information to give you the tools needed to start an effective mindfulness practice, begin to reap the benefits, and be an informed consumer of mindfulness training.

Part II is a deeper dive into mindfulness (and some non-mindfulness) exercises to begin to create a consistent practice so you can move from merely an intellectual understanding of mindfulness to an embodied knowledge that positively affects your experience. Part II is meant to be followed as an 8-week course in which you read the content of week 1 and do the exercises outlined at the end of the chapter for a *minimum* of 1 week, before moving on to week 2 and beyond.

Here is a quick overview of the 8-week course:

Week 1: No Trivial Moments: Moving from Autopilot to Aware
Week 2: The Mindset You Bring to Your Experience Matters
Week 3: Do You Have the Story or Does the Story Have You?
Week 4: The Saber-Toothed Tiger of the Modern World: Everything
Week 5: Delving into the Difficult
Week 6: In the Same Boat
Week 7: Who Watches (Out for) You?
Week 8: Maintaining Momentum

Getting the most out of this book requires a commitment to doing the practices consistently. It's fine if you want to read the entire book first to get a sense of things and then actually do the course later, but do not lie to yourself as you close the last page and think, "I got this; now I know how to be mindful." If you do that, you'll be about as mindful as one of those rocks in a Zen garden. You'd only have an intellectual understanding of mindfulness, which is pretty much useless. Whether you are new to mindfulness or have a long-term practice, I encourage you to start at the beginning of the book and work your way through in chapter order, doing the exercises consistently along the way. Practice is the only way to reap the benefits of mindfulness. Let's get to it.

Part I

My Journey with Mindfulness and an Introduction to the Fundamentals

Chapter 1

The Power of the Trained Mind

On June 13, 1994, I stepped off a bus at Fort Jackson, South Carolina, and was immediately assailed by the shouts from a group of US Army drill sergeants. As you might imagine, my heart was pounding in my chest and I was thinking, "What the hell did I get myself into?" I had barely made the grades needed to graduate from high school just 3 days prior and this was the first step on what has turned out to be an incredible journey through life with its ups, downs, and hard-won lessons learned. I had many family members who served our country and inspired me to do the same, and I wanted to "earn my freedom," a phrase which, as it turned out, had two meanings.

The first meaning of "earn my freedom" was recognizing I won the world lottery by being born in the United States of America but had done absolutely nothing to earn it. Serving my country was one way to do so. I grew up being inspired by my Uncle Ernie, who served in the US Marines during the Vietnam War and later joined the Army, where he served until retirement. Every Christmas Eve at my grandmother's house in Gettysburg, Pennsylvania, we would gather around the phone for our chance to talk with Ernie for a few minutes when he called in from a far-off place. There was always talk about service, patriotism, and sacrifice after we hung up that phone each year. Those sentiments instilled in me a desire to earn my freedom, and Ernie's stories kindled my interest in leaving my small town to explore the world.

The second meaning of "earn my freedom" came from the fact that we were dirt poor, and earning my financial freedom was high on my list of to-dos. I learned at a very young age what many kids

3

do not learn until later in life, sometimes much later, that the food that arrived on my table each night and the roof over my head were there due to others sacrificing and laboring for me when I could do little in return. Crossing that threshold of understanding about the world fueled my motivation to become self-reliant, claw my way out of poverty, and help others.

Joining the US Army was one of the most important and impactful decisions of my life. The self-discipline, friendships, and experiences I gained in the Army shaped who I am, carried me through challenging times, helped me find the courage to take personal and physical risks, helped me get into and graduate from Harvard, and continue to fuel my motivation to serve others today. But I needed far more than just my experiences in the Army to move from poverty to prosperity.

My journey has not been linear by any stretch of the imagination. I was raised by a single mother of three. We were on and off welfare for much of my childhood, moved nearly a dozen times and across several states, lived in government-subsidized housing, a trailer park, and even had to stay in a shelter for a time when things went sideways with my mom's boyfriend. At Christmas time, we often got free toys from Toys for Tots,[1] and during much of my time in school, we were on a free or reduced-cost lunch plan, which required the issuance, carrying, and "spending" of lunch tokens daily in the cafeteria. Noticing my cheeks turn bright red and dealing with intense feelings of embarrassment and shame when a classmate pointed out that I was getting free lunches was an all-too-common occurrence in my school. These circumstances kept me feeling small, feeling like a failure, and wondering why everyone else had it better than I did.

I was not, you might agree, set up for success. That said, I did not lack love and attention from my mother nor good examples of hard work, discipline, and the importance of family from her, as well as my aunts, uncles, and grandparents. I remember my mother working tirelessly to make ends meet while operating her station on the production line in a shoe factory, which was kind of a family profession back then. My grandparents moved from coal mine country in West Virginia to work at Gettysburg Shoe, in Gettysburg, Pennsylvania. Everyone in my extended family worked factory or other laborious jobs. Their collars weren't blue; their entire shirt was. Other than my Uncle Ernie, who was one of the main inspirations for me joining the military, the adult family members who surrounded me worked in shoe factories, cabinet factories, dinnerware factories, and quarries.

They drove trucks, welded bars, sawed wood, and laid brick. All jobs that were much better than breathing in coal dust like my great grandfather.

My mother bore the brunt of raising us in difficult times, but there was much I'm sure I didn't see because she shielded it from my siblings and me. After each long day's work, my mom would pick us up from the babysitter's house and give us her full attention, ask about our day, and shower us with love. When I was old enough to go to school the schedule changed a bit, and in third grade, I became a latchkey kid. My mother's affection didn't wane, and she always came up with ways to give us opportunities she knew she couldn't provide on her own. One day she heard about a contest for low-income families to win free martial arts lessons at our local martial arts studio, So's Tae Kwon Do.[2] She knew, from the stacks of old kung fu magazines and my penchant for wanting to watch every Chuck Norris and Bruce Lee movie a hundred times, that I would kill (pun intended) for a chance to actually learn martial arts and so she entered me into the contest. She didn't tell me about it before getting the results because she knew how devastated I'd be if we didn't win. Fortunately, I was one of the five lucky kids who won and although the free lessons were to last only two months, the owner and head instructor, Grandmaster Chong C. So, was an amazingly generous man. He was the architect of the contest and when he heard my mother was going to cancel "cable and HBO" to pay for my lessons to continue, he said he would keep teaching me for free as long as I was committed to the training (see Figures 1.1 and 1.2). I spent the next two years or so taking free lessons and, although it wasn't explicitly labeled mindfulness, Master So also taught us focused attention meditation and how to be aware of some often-overlooked aspects of our experience as we trained, competed, and navigated day-to-day life. I picked up three things in that program that I carried forward in my life that have helped me thrive.

Three Skills That Changed My Life

The first skill Master So taught us was to recognize, embrace, and be mindful of the sensations and thoughts associated with fear and then still step forward. "What does fear feel like in the body?" and "How does fear show up in the mind?" were questions Master So posed to us. We learned to exercise this skill each time we approached the sparring mat and faced a stronger or more advanced opponent.

FIGURE 1.1 PICTURE OF ME AT SO'S TAE KWON DO TAKING A TEST FOR MY NEXT BELT LEVEL. I'M THE KID ON THE RIGHT ALTHOUGH THE CAPTION SAYS LEFT.

Source: The Evening Sun, 29 August 1986. © Shirley Sherry – USA TODAY NETWORK.

Notice the fear, and move forward. Notice the hesitation, and move forward. Notice the heart racing, and move forward. It was by turning toward and embracing fear that we learned we could do anything, whether fear was present or not.

The second skill Master So taught was to be mindful of unhelpful internal thoughts, beliefs, and stories and still move forward despite their presence. These are the automatic thoughts that tell us we aren't good enough, tall enough, or smart enough. They often claim we don't belong, some achievements are only for others, or other people have it better and that's why they're successful, keeping us in a victim mentality. That unhelpful inner dialogue also includes rumination and worry, far in excess of any helpful contemplation of how to face and overcome a challenge or difficult situation. We learned to exercise this skill each time we had to break wooden boards and eventually cement blocks with specific strikes, such as hammer fist or knife hand strikes. As a young boy about to attempt these types of breaks, my mind would race with thoughts of "I can't do this. There are too many. It's going hurt." Notice the unhelpful thinking; do the action anyway. Each time we did this, we reinforced our ability to move forward despite a weak and fearful mind, which eventually gave way to a stronger one.

Two plan to keep taking free lessons

Early this summer, So stated in an article in *The Evening Sun* that he would like to give two months of free lessons to five low-income youth.

Twenty applied and he chose five, but only two kept at it — Matthew Dehoff, a seventh-grader at Emory Markle Middle School, and Tom Smith, a fifth-grader at Hanover Street School.

Both boys said they had "always wanted" to take the lessons.

"My mom told me she would get rid of cable and HBO to keep me in lessons," Smith said.

She won't have to lose her television entertainment, for So has said he will keep teaching the boys as long as they keep practicing. Both come in three times a week for classes.

"I'd like to teach them until they get their black belts and can be teachers. Then I will tell them they must each teach one other child who is in the low-income category," he said.

"I think they will both finish — they really want to learn — and I hope they will be honest about keeping their promise," he said.

FIGURE 1.2 EXCERPT FROM THE SAME ARTICLE DISCUSSING THE CONTEST FOR LOW-INCOME KIDS AND MY MOM'S OFFER TO CUT CABLE AND HBO SO I COULD KEEP TAKING LESSONS.
Source: The Evening Sun, 29 August 1986. © Shirley Sherry – USA TODAY NETWORK.

This skill of becoming aware of unhelpful thoughts and not letting them affect my actions was reinforced by something my Uncle Howard said when we were fishing one afternoon. He said, "Tommy (that's what everyone called me back then), one thing I love about fishing is that you can cast your line into the water and just let all your worries flow down the stream." At the time, I did not fully grasp the wisdom of this comment. What's most surprising about it, as I've looked back on that interaction, is that the comment was uttered by a mountain man with a big heart, who had lived his entire life in an area outside Gettysburg, Pennsylvania, called "the Narrows." He shared an insight with me that he didn't have to travel to an exotic land to discover, didn't have to kiss the feet of a guru to gain access to, and didn't have to take on the demeanor, political views, or values of someone else to be considered worthy of learning it. He shared that nugget with me not knowing if I was ready to hear it and not expecting anything in return. He planted the seed and helped me learn to notice that the world has lessons to teach if we only pay attention. And that wasn't the only nugget of wisdom fishing yielded in support of this skill.

Every time we went fishing, we did something called "catch and release." No, it wasn't a controversial immigration tactic; it was what we did every time we caught a fish. Catch a bass, release it. Catch trout, release it. You get the picture. I turned this phrase into a way to practice the second skill outside the martial arts studio.

The Catch and Release technique became (and remains) one of my most powerful tools for noticing and letting go of unhelpful internal dialogue and fear-driven thinking. Suddenly, I could do the things I was afraid of and attempt the things my mind told me I couldn't do. I would "catch" myself buying into an unhelpful thought and "release" it and any automatic impulse to believe or follow it. "I'm not good enough." Catch and Release it. "I'll never learn this." Catch and Release it. "If only we were rich, then we'd be happy." Catch and Release it. This one technique alone can massively change your life.

The third skill we learned came as a direct outcome of Master So requiring we regularly practice focused attention meditation, which I describe in Chapter 6. This exercise cultivated an ability to focus our attention at will and keep it where we wanted it to be, even under the stress and duress of sparring. I must admit this skill was much easier to learn back in the mid-1980s before everyone had a super-computer in their pocket and access to entertainment 24 hours a day, 7 days a week.

Just as fishing yielded insights and skills associated with mindfulness, I was able to practice a manner of focused attention meditation throughout my teenage years through another outdoor activity. I had some amazing uncles, cousins, and family friends who would take me hunting regularly. Sitting in the woods in 30-degree temperatures, with only your breath keeping you company, while waiting for a deer to step into a clearing, is a fantastic way to cultivate the power of concentration (as well as patience and the subtle art of not complaining).

Once a deer does step into your field of view, your body is immediately flooded with adrenalin, your heart starts pounding out of your chest, and yet you must remain calm, quiet, and steady if you want that deer to feed your family for a few months.

Those three core mindfulness skills, as well as some insights I learned along my journey, became crucial when opportunities crossed my path as you'll soon see.

The Three Skills Applied

That first skill of being aware of fear and moving forward despite that fear became extremely useful early in my career. When I flew to Fort Jackson, South Carolina, the day I left for the Army, it was the first time I ever flew in a plane. I quickly discovered I was absolutely terrified of flying and heights. This was the kind of terrifying experience when you can hardly breathe, you're white-knuckling the arms of the seat, and sweat beads up on your forehead. I can attest that flight attendants ask you if you are okay when you display that level of fear.

Thankfully, I got through that initial flight but realized this level of fear of flying was something I would want to overcome to fully experience this life and our world. So, when I had an opportunity to go to Airborne School and "learn" to jump out of airplanes, I leaned into that fear and volunteered. It was a profound experience to be totally consumed by fear in my body and thoughts, still jump (fall!) out of that plane, and be okay on the other side of the experience. When you learn you can feel high levels of fear and still consistently move forward despite it, no goal is out of reach.

The second skill—being aware of unhelpful inner dialogue/ self-talk and not allowing it to dissuade me or negatively impact on outcomes—came to the fore when I was considering reenlisting in the Army as my first term was coming to a close. Of the jobs available, one jumped out at me as interesting: linguist. The Army had a significant need for speakers of a number of languages, including Russian, Vietnamese, Chinese, Arabic, Korean, and a few more. It was the Chinese linguist position that caught my eye.

Now, if you think the guy who graduated in what was probably the bottom third of his high school class had some negative self-talk about his intellectual capabilities, you'd be right. There were thoughts that arose saying, "You never did well in Spanish!" and "Don't you remember you FAILED high school English, your *native* language, and had to retake it in order to graduate; do you really think you can learn one of the hardest languages on the planet?!" Yet in that moment I was able to Catch and Release those unhelpful thoughts and attempt to do the thing I wanted to do.

The next step in the process was to take a test to gauge my aptitude, which objectively reported that I had an aptitude for learning difficult languages, such as Arabic, Chinese, Vietnamese, and so on. However, similar to the staggered start situation, this was another instance when I had objective information saying one thing but internally I still felt the opposite. My mind was still saying, "I can't learn Chinese; I couldn't even learn Spanish." So, what did I do? I chose to try to learn Chinese. If I could learn this language despite the incessant whining and fear-based thinking that was automatically coming up, I could do anything!

I soon arrived at the Defense Language Institute (DLI) in Monterey, California, the military's premier school for turning out fluent linguists. Fortunately, I was blissfully unaware of the 50% to 70% attrition rate, which would have only reinforced all the unhelpful internal dialogue I was already experiencing.

The Chinese Mandarin Basic Course was actually 63 weeks of intense training and was anything but "basic." I was in a class of 30 people, and we were broken down into individual groups of 10 for our direct instruction; there's no sitting in the back of the room hiding your way through this type of training.

I started this course with a determination and drive I'd never felt previously in my life. I spent the entire first third of the course busting my tail, studying for 2 to 3 hours after an 8-hour day of classroom instruction. It was a challenging schedule but I wasn't going to fail due to not trying hard enough. When I got my grades the first trimester, I was crestfallen. All my hard work, the 10- to 11-hour days, the intense studying in my room without distraction, the hundreds of flashcards I made by hand (there were no phone apps back in 1997) and practiced with for hours on the weekends, had yielded only B pluses across all evaluated areas.

Yes, you read that correctly. Let that sink in for a moment. I tried the hardest I'd ever tried to do anything in my life to learn one of the most difficult languages on Earth. I got B pluses on my first report card, and I was—crestfallen? Wouldn't a better automatic reaction have been an inner thought that said something like, "OMG you failed high school English like four years ago and you just got B pluses in the Chinese course at one of the most premier language schools on the planet!!!" I think that would have been better, but what did my brain do? What all brains do; it looked for and highlighted the negative—I didn't earn a B plus, I missed an A. We'll talk more about focusing on what we are missing versus what we have and its impact later, but at this point, I had become quite wary of the inner critic; it was as if he was primarily operating from a place of fear and worry.

I had a choice to make in that moment. I'd busted my tail and received B pluses and had not really socialized much outside of Friday and Saturday evenings. I had made some awesome friends, who are still some of my best friends today—Eric,[3] Chris, and Heidi—but I wasn't really spending much time with them. So, I Caught and Released the self-criticism about being a failure and not trying hard enough, and I decided maybe I was trying too hard.

The analogy I came up with, when trying to understand why my extreme effort wasn't enough, was related to driving. When learning to drive, it was much harder when I was younger and had a death grip on the steering wheel because of the strong sense it would help me be more in control of the situation. It wasn't until I learned to loosen the grip a bit that the ride and my driving became much smoother. Maybe the way I was going about learning Chinese was all wrong? So, I lifted my foot off the throttle a bit and began spending some time with my friends during the week, adding some balance to my life. I still studied each night but my decision not only brought more balance to my life but also resulted in a major shift in how I treated myself while studying.

Of my three closest friends at DLI, Heidi was a student in the Chinese class a few weeks behind mine. Meaning, when I was on Lesson 10, she was on Lesson 7. We began to study together to get through the homework and learn more effectively.

One of the dreaded homework assignments our teachers inflicted on us regularly was dubbed "rapid-fire." We had to translate sentences recorded in Chinese on cassette tapes (yes, they were still in use then), but the recordings were not what you might expect in your average Spanish or French class: crystal clear audio and perfect pronunciation. No, these were garbled commands seemingly shouted across a crowded fish market toward another human facing in the opposite direction. It also seemed to be sped up to 150% normal speed. It was brutal. No one liked doing rapid-fire. It's like doing squats; you know it's helpful but it burns like hell and sometimes you throw up. I learned, though, it wasn't so bad doing the rapid-fire homework the second time around with Heidi.

I would do my rapid-fire homework then help Heidi work through her sentences, which I had completed 3 weeks prior. Listening to those sentences the second time around, I wasn't so rigid with stress and striving to make sure I got every single word. I relaxed, let go, and just listened. I soon realized I could capture more of the sentences with less effort, which began to improve my confidence and trust in my abilities. But the real kicker, the powerful insight that changed my life, was I began to notice what I said to Heidi if she made a mistake versus what I said to myself when I made a mistake.

My comments to her were filled with understanding and kindness. They were tinged with encouragement and care. The entire communication from me to her was enveloped in patience, empathy, and warmth, with a dash of humor. In contrast to my communications style toward Heidi, my inner critic treated my mistakes, missteps, and failures as proof I wasn't cut out for learning Chinese, that I'd fail, and was an idiot for making certain "simple" mistakes. I decided to do something different.

After Catching and Releasing unhelpful thoughts that would automatically arise after a mistake or when facing a challenging situation, I decided to follow up with a question. I would ask myself, "How would I respond to this mistake if I were teaching someone else this subject?" The response was never, "Hey, idiot, you're going to fail at this!" It was always a much more compassionate and supportive response. I wasn't trying to delude myself; I still needed to learn the language and graduate from the course. Empty platitudes weren't going to help. However, this approach enabled me to shift from self-attack to self-compassion.

After 63 weeks of people speaking Mandarin Chinese to me for 8-plus hours a day, and a great deal of studying with some of the best friends I've ever had, I graduated from DLI with honors, held the highest GPA of my cohort at 3.7, and scored the highest reading grade on our final test, prompting one of our native Chinese teachers to comment, "I couldn't score that high on a Chinese reading test."

I proved to myself that my inner critic didn't know what the hell he was talking about. In fact, I decided, if my inner critic says I can't do something, I'm going to go for the most challenging, interesting, and/or exciting option. I basically started treating my inner critic like that guy we all have in our office who thinks he knows everything, he has the "inside track" on how the new policy sucks and it's going to be bad, but when you check on anything he says it's wrong, and so you decide to humor him when he talks to you or warns you about something, and then you just go on with the rest of your day thinking nothing of it again. When you learn you don't have to believe what you say to yourself about yourself, the world opens up for you.

As you might imagine I gained a bit of self-confidence as my grades in the Chinese program improved and certainly later when I graduated. It was at this point in my career I decided I wanted to work toward obtaining a college degree. As I mentioned, I graduated from high school on a Friday and was flying to an Army base on Monday, so I didn't go to college. I had an option to use some of my DLI training to support getting an associate's degree and I could begin while still at DLI, so I took some classes while in Chinese language training and earned an AA degree in language from Monterey Peninsula College.[4] And later, while I was assigned to Schofield Barracks in Hawaii, I looked for a program online that I could take while still working full time as an active duty soldier. No one in my family had a bachelor's degree and I wanted to break that cycle, but the only way I would be able to do it was if I made a sacrifice in some of my downtime to focus on chipping away at this goal. I pursued a bachelor of science degree in business information systems at Bellevue University.[5] It took me a few years of working at night during my different assignments in the Army, but by carving out the time needed to get the work done, I graduated with honors and became the first person in my family to get a bachelor's degree. When I learned to regularly prioritize time for self-development and self-care, I realized some goals just required consistent application of effort over time as opposed to high levels of natural talent or wealth.

■ ■ ■

My Army career took me across the US from the East Coast all the way to Hawaii, with many states in between, and then back to Maryland to work at Fort Meade doing signals intelligence collection work, listening to foreign communications, and translating conversations. This was when I first volunteered to deploy to the Middle East during Operations Enduring Freedom and Iraqi Freedom. In 2003, I left the Army after nearly 10 years but continued to serve my country by joining the Defense Intelligence Agency (DIA) as a civilian intelligence officer where I served for 7 years.

After successfully working my way through a series of the intelligence community's (IC's) increasingly complex and the single-most-challenging human intelligence collection courses, where I learned to gather intelligence from the most complex entities, humans, I began my career in one of the riskiest professions the IC has to offer: espionage. I volunteered again to deploy and served tours in Afghanistan and Iraq with some of the most selfless and under-recognized patriots our country has protecting us at the tip of the spear.

Although you might think all that seems interesting and exciting, and it was, my crowning assignment with DIA wasn't in a war zone. After coming back from Iraq in 2007, I had an opportunity to go to the Joint Military Attaché School, where DIA personnel go to learn to be diplomats and how to navigate the maneuvering and double-talk associated with diplomacy. On completing the training, I was selected to become a diplomat and represent my country in an assignment at the US Embassy in Beijing, China.

Given my journey thus far, a poor kid from the wrong side of the tracks joins the Army as an enlisted soldier, learns Chinese, gets educated, and eventually becomes a diplomat, representing our country with one of the most important strategic and often contentious foreign relationships we have, you might imagine this was the pinnacle of my career up to that point in my life. It was. You'd also probably think I was on top of the world, and I was, outwardly. I mean, I displayed that excitement. Inwardly, though, I still had some of those self-defeating thoughts popping into my head from time to time which still took diligent effort to Catch and Release.

Not long after meeting all the brilliant and highly educated professionals assigned to the US Embassy Beijing, I began to have more and more thoughts making me feel like I didn't belong, like I was an imposter, and that I would soon be found out when I had to face a tough question. These thoughts were a little more difficult to Catch and Release because they weren't coming up in automatic response to some specific external challenge. Instead, they were coming up more subtly in response to an overall awareness that the folks I worked with were pretty amazing, had done so many interesting things, and went to schools like Harvard, Princeton, Yale, Brown, and Columbia.

So, when an embassy colleague suggested I apply to Harvard when I began considering attending graduate school, I told him he was out of his <bleeping> mind. I immediately shared, "I barely graduated high school and, oh yeah, I have an online undergraduate degree." I explained it would be a colossal waste of time and money. Plus applying to Harvard is like doing your taxes in exchange for one lottery ticket and you have to wait three months to hear the winning numbers. But doing your taxes is actually a lot easier than applying to Harvard. My Catch and Release system was offline. I wasn't catching anything; I was totally taken in by the story created by my thinking.

Consider for a moment the arc of my career as I've described it thus far. I don't presume to know how you define success in your life, and I certainly don't think success is merely achievement after achievement (we could have an entire book on the futility of seeking happiness/fulfilment through external achievement). However, it was pretty clear at that point in my life, I had enough evidence showing that even if I was afraid or if some aspiration seemed or felt impossible, it did not mean it actually was impossible. For example, if I had succumbed to fear and believed negative self-talk up to that point, I would have never jumped out of planes, learned Chinese, or done a number of other things I have to leave out due to the security classification level of those activities. Yet, here I was having my brain automatically serve up all these limiting beliefs about applying to Harvard.

Why might my brain serve up those thoughts despite ample evidence to the contrary and a robust Catch and Release system? Well, as I've discovered, and reams of research bears this out, our brains aren't designed to make us happy; they are designed to keep us safe and ensure we survive. So, in that situation, my brain automatically began predicting what would happen if I took the chance to apply to Harvard and the answer it came to was this: "This effort will lead to failure." What does failure equal? Failure equals pain from our brain's point of view. Therefore, my brain served up the belief that this was impossible and added in self-talk such as "Don't even try; who do you think you are?" "It'll be embarrassing when you fail." "Let's just move on to something more realistic." Why those thoughts? Because those beliefs and automatic thoughts might nudge me to take actions (or refrain from taking actions) that would avoid failure (avoid pain) and would serve to keep me in my comfort zone (keep me feeling safe). They would also keep me from taking a chance.

Fortunately for me, my colleague asked a number of times over the following three weeks, whether I had applied to Harvard yet. Thankfully, Catch and Release finally kicked in! I let the inner critic have his say, I let go, and asked myself, "If I was able to meet the previous 'impossible' challenges in my life, why not this one, too?" The response I got was, "You may not be able to control the outcome of getting accepted or not, but you can refrain from ruling yourself out and can control the effort you put into the application." Those thoughts led me to take the leap and apply to Harvard. A few months later, much to my surprise and delight, I opened an email from Harvard University's John F. Kennedy School of Government on April 8,

2010, and the first word read, "Congratulations!" It really did feel like I won the lottery but the odds were much better than what my mind was telling me.

What I learned from that entire experience was that we can either be pushed around by and blindly believe every thought that bubbles up in our head or we can see thoughts for what they are, just thoughts. Sometimes thoughts are true, sometimes partially true, and sometimes they are totally false. I also learned that engaging with others is a great way to check our automatic judgments and benefit from other perspectives we may be overlooking. This inspired me to become an executive coach and to teach mindfulness, because they are such powerful tools to uncover and transcend our limiting beliefs and other psychological barriers to success, which opens us up to the opportunities we all come across throughout our lives.

●   ●   ■

This is one journey I hope can show you: it's not the past that determines the future; it's the present that determines the future. Mindfulness keeps us in the present moment when we can fully interact with and affect our lives. Where you came from, what your mom or dad said to you when you were little, your socioeconomic status as a kid, or what other people had that you didn't or don't have don't determine whether or not you thrive in this life. It's what you choose to focus on, to develop and do today, in this moment, that determines the quality of your life.

Sure, we can go through life believing thoughts such as "If I had what she had growing up then I'd be where she is" or "Of course he's successful; he was born with a silver spoon in his mouth" or "There's no way someone like me could ever achieve that." But the cost of indulging in the "comparing mind" and believing those self-limiting thoughts is that it will keep you miserable, in a victim mentality, and in your comfort zone. Is your brain keeping you in your comfort zone? *Your comfort zone is where your dreams go to die.* It's only by pushing to the edges of our comfort zone and beyond that we can set and achieve goals that stretch us to grow beyond what our thoughts typically tell us about what we can accomplish.

The Army was the first place I got to test out those three mindfulness skills. My time in the military also played a big role in helping me develop a healthy level of self-discipline. It enabled me to connect with individuals with high standards I could aspire to emulate, it showed me the relationship between effort and outcome, it gave me an additional framework of values from which to guide much of my behavior and decisions, and it helped me see the amazing benefits of a life in service to others.

You can start to cultivate those three mindfulness skills wherever you are; you don't have to join the military. Joining the Army just happened to be my first decision on a journey in which many might say I was dealt a "bad hand" from initial life/family circumstances and I could have just folded. I don't think anyone would have blamed me, and I could have used my socioeconomic status as a kid as an excuse to stay small and complain my entire life away. Instead, over time, I learned to play the hand I was dealt and have learned to enjoy the journey, including the ups and the downs. I've tried not to spend too much time complaining about the dealer (God, the universe, parents, bosses), blaming the shuffle (fate, randomness), or looking at other people's cards (people more fortunate than me). None of those things ever helps in the long run.

Instead, enjoy the game, bluff on occasion, and don't be afraid to go all in from time to time. Life does deal us a set of cards in the beginning that we cannot change, but we get to make our own decisions about how we are going to respond to life; mindfulness moves us from automatic reaction to thoughtful response.

Furthermore, we all, every single one of us, get dealt opportunity cards from time to time. We can use those opportunities as catalysts for change on our journey if we are present enough to see them, mindful enough of our internal talk to go after them, and compassionate enough to dust ourselves off after our inevitable stumbles, missteps, and failures (aka learning opportunities).

Like my Uncle Howard, who shared his insights with no strings attached, I promise to do the same. I won't lecture you on what you should or shouldn't believe. I won't subtly imply your political views aren't the right ones. I won't suggest you need to buy a bell, a little statue of the Buddha, or a string of rudraksha beads to learn and benefit from mindfulness. I offer you the following knowledge, insights, and practices to plant seeds and give you tools that can enable you to transcend limiting beliefs, achieve your dreams, and navigate life with a bit more ease.

■ ■ ■

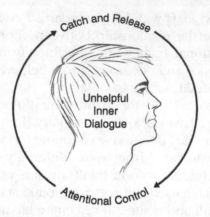

FIGURE 1.3 CATCH AND RELEASE.

Source: From 99designs.com/Konstantin. Reprinted with permission of 99designs.com.

Many people never finish the books they start reading. If you are one of those people, no worries, but I want you to walk away with the three key takeaways from this chapter that, if adhered to, will greatly affect your life. You must learn to focus and control your attention. If you don't, someone else will (or already has control of it). It is the foundation on which everything else rests. You must learn to become more aware of internal dialogue and how it affects your state of mind and life. If you are lost in your internal dialogue, you are ruled by it. Finally, use Catch and Release to break the chains of control your inner dialogue has on you. These three skills are mutually reinforcing. Increased ability to command your own attention helps you notice unhelpful internal dialogue, noticing allows you to Catch and Release it, loosening its grip on you, which enables you to more easily command your attention. See Figure 1.3 for an illustration of this process.

Chapter 2

Why Mindfulness Now?

Every year, I teach mindfulness to thousands of corporate workers, senior executives, business owners, and government officials who, by any measure on this planet, are extremely successful people. Most of them have gotten to where they are in their professional lives without a daily mindfulness practice. It's just as likely that you, too, dear reader, have gotten to wherever you are in your life without practicing mindfulness. Why would successful leaders in business or government want to change their approach now, after it's been so fruitful? Why should you? What's different? Why add another thing to what is likely an already overwhelming to-do list?

I think there is value in stepping into the world of business transformation for a moment and seeing what companies are doing today as a way to draw some parallels to our individual situations. According to Marketsandmarkets.com, a business-to-business research and market intelligence firm, the digital transformation market was expected to grow from $290 billion in 2018 to $665 billion by 2023.[1] Why would companies spend such massive amounts of money transforming their business models? In a word, disruption.

It's not lost on company leaders that corporate survivability, a phrase describing the ability of a company to withstand disruption, crisis, or other factors negatively affecting the business, is declining. An Innosight.com executive briefing titled "Corporate Longevity: Turbulence Ahead for Large Organizations" describes the reduced tenure companies can expect to enjoy on the S&P 500.[2] According to the report, in 1965 companies averaged 33 years listed on the S&P 500. By 1990 the average shrunk to just 20 years. The projection for

2026: 14 years. This is enough of a trend to make credible business leaders pay attention and take steps to ensure their company remains viable and strong. What's happening? Massive technological change.

The volume and velocity of change, innovation, information, and disruption companies must manage today has never before been seen on this planet. Recent history is littered with failed companies that did not adjust to the new realities of a rapidly advancing technological world. Remember Blockbuster? Kodak? Radio Shack? Borders bookstores? The message is clear to businesses: if you do not transform to meet the realities of the present, you'll become a "what not to do" case study at Harvard Business School.

Here are some of the major innovations and changes companies are currently adapting to or working to incorporate into their business models:

- ◆ Artificial intelligence
- ◆ Machine learning
- ◆ Blockchain technology
- ◆ Augmented reality
- ◆ Virtual reality
- ◆ Cloud computing
- ◆ 5G
- ◆ Internet of things
- ◆ Remote working technology (In 2020 as I write this many people have been working from home due to the COVID-19 pandemic, forcing companies to adopt this technology quickly.)
- ◆ Advanced persistent threats in cybersecurity

The list goes on and, therefore, we have a multi-hundred-billion-dollar market opportunity each year in the digital transformation space for professional consulting firms to help usher companies through these transformations, not so businesses merely survive these rapid technological changes but so they thrive within them.

Do we really think that we, as individuals, are not affected by the changes of the modern world? The volume and velocity of change, information, and disruption we each face is massively different than it was just 20, 10, or even only 5 years ago. Work demands on individuals' "off" time are significantly higher today, causing an increased blurring of work time and family or personal time. There is also a nearly constant barrage of attempts to hijack our attention in this new "attention economy" in which companies have learned to capture, maintain, and monetize our attention.[3] We face a crisis of complexity and a disaster of distraction.

If you are honest with yourself, you are probably in the following situation: your work and work-related activities get the bulk of your attention. One or two apps on your phone get another huge helping of attention. A compelling TV series on Netflix gets a nice portion. After all that, your spouse/partner, children, other family members, and friends get what's left over, and what they get is quite fragmented. How did we get here?

▪ ▪ ▪

The first smartphone available for purchase by consumers was the IBM Simon Personal Communicator in 1994, but only about 50,000 units were sold in the 6 months it was available before being pulled from the market.[4] Although it boasted cutting-edge mobile capabilities such as a calendar, calculator, fax, mail, and notepad, among others, its approximately 1-hour battery life left users wanting.[5] It wasn't until 2002 that Canadian company Research in Motion (RIM) unleashed the BlackBerry onto the world stage and kicked off the shift from working only while at work to working from anywhere. The BlackBerry revolutionized work email as its salespeople did an exceptional job convincing corporate leaders and IT managers to allow their servers to push email to the devices of millions of professional workers regardless of their location. Executives could now check their email at work, at home, in the train station, at the bar, and in a restaurant. How convenient.

The device became so popular among the corporate elite that only 3 years later in 2005, CNN was reporting that "the telltale signs of BlackBerry addiction are everywhere."[6] The report later predicted, "As BlackBerry use spreads so, inevitably, will the complaints about over-worked, addicted professionals who just can't put the gadgets down." RIM founder, Mike Lazaridi, quoted in the article, said, "The person that means a lot to me that complains the most loudly about my BlackBerry use is my wife. I realized a lot of executives were having the same problem so I came up with the perfect solution. I gave her one too, and I suggested they do the same."[7]

In 2005, an average of only 23 received emails per day by businesspeople led to spouses complaining,[8] journalists reporting on potential addiction, and researchers investigating the impact of emails on work-related overload and burnout. Oh, my, how times have changed. I'd kill to receive only 23 emails a day! We didn't have a clue what was to come. Just 10 years later in 2015, that number rose to 88 business emails received, and the average sent was 24, for a total of 122 emails per day.[9]

In 2007, the iPhone took the world by storm, kicking off the real smartphone race, which eventually led to smartphones with email, web browsing, and social media apps in the hands of billions of people, not just those in corporate settings. Fast forward to today and not only do we have the email situation to contend with but also we consume media and social media at rates that make 2005 seem like the most relaxing time in our history.

In 2019, adults in the US spent an average of 12 hours and 9 minutes per day consuming media, with the breakdown as follows: 6 hours and 35 minutes on digital media, 3 hours and 35 minutes on TV, 11 minutes reading newspapers, and 9 minutes reading magazines.[10] Let that sink in a moment. We spend over half of our 24 hours per day consuming media. What must this mean? Well, we are either doing all of our sleeping, working, eating, showering, conversing, and so on in the remaining 12 hours *or* we are consuming a great deal of media while doing other things, aka "multitasking."

This is the world we live in now. A world where we continuously try to do multiple things simultaneously. Therefore, we do most of them worse than we would if we'd just focus on one thing at a time. But we don't feel like we have enough time to do all the things we want or need to do, so in an effort to be productive and efficient we push the gas pedal even more, pull all-nighters, sacrifice family time, and/or reduce our time sleeping. Gloria Mark, a professor in the Department of Infomatics at University of California, Irvine, is one the of world's most prominent experts on the impact of human–technology interaction.[11] One of her key areas of study is on email use in the workplace and how distraction and multitasking affect things such as mood, stress, and perceived productivity. Her bottom line, as quoted in *The Globe and Mail* in 2014, was, "Digital activity is a boon to us, but it's not without its costs. The cost is stress and disruption of focus. We aren't as productive as we might be."[12] I would add on to that last statement: "even though it feels like we are being more productive."

That last part may be shocking to some. You might be asking right now, "Wait, do you mean to say I'm not as productive when I'm multitasking?" My response is absolutely, but it's not that simple. Multitasking might actually lead to getting an individual task done in less time but not because you were more efficient. For example, let's say you had to prepare a work paper for your boss and you have 60 minutes to do it. After 15 minutes of work on the paper, you switch your screen to an online ticket merchant to try to get concert tickets as soon as they are available for sale online. You switch back to your work paper a few times but it takes you 30 minutes to get the tickets. You come back to the work paper and have 15 minutes until it's due so you rush through and turn it in but the quality is not your best. So, yeah, in that case, you did actually get the work paper task done in 30 minutes versus the full 60 you had available but what's the impact on the quality? Perhaps you didn't actually need the entire 60 minutes anyway, but switching tasks certainly had an impact on what you could have produced had you just stuck to each of the tasks separately to completion. Examples of this have been tested in the lab with compelling results. Stephen Monsell, a researcher at the University of Exeter, reviewed extensive research on task switching (including his own) showing when people switched between even simple tasks, they took longer on the tasks and made more mistakes, which was dubbed "switch cost."[13] Furthermore, even when people were prepared ahead of time, such as they knew the switch was coming and what the new task would be, there was still a switch cost, albeit a reduced one.

What the research is telling us is that multitasking is a myth. We aren't actually focused on two (or more) things at once and being super-productive and efficient. Instead we are just single-tasking back and forth between tasks (aka context switching), giving each task intermittent attention to the detriment of our goal of efficiency. What feels like productive activity is actually one of the most inefficient ways of working.

In the context of the modern world it's a rather dire situation. We are constantly bombarded by email notifications, text messages, and social media pings indicating our recent post garnered yet another "like" and comment. Similar to ship captains mesmerized by sirens' songs luring them into shallow waters to crash on hidden rocks, we are seduced by sounds of the smartphone, dashing us on the rocks of distraction and pulling us under the water of wasted time. Those "quick checks" of email or social media have their own cost beyond inefficiency. Research by Gloria Mark published back in 2004 and 2005 showed office workers were interrupted or self-interrupted every 3 minutes, and it took them over 23 minutes, on average, to get back on their original task after they had been interrupted.[14] Not only is "multitasking" making you less efficient with your time and more likely to make errors but your work is interrupted every 3 minutes and it's taking you nearly a half-hour to get back to the thing you were working on in the first place. What do you think that is going to do for your ability to get back into the flow of whatever you were working on after such a long break? Speaking of breaks, let's make a quick distinction. Taking a break, a real break, such as going on a 15-minute walk outside after working 60 minutes straight on a project is very helpful. That's not what we are talking about here. Checking your social media feed every 15 minutes isn't a "break," at least not from your brain's point of view. In fact, it's more likely to ramp up your stress levels.[15]

It's amazing we get anything accomplished at all. The scary part of this whole situation is that it isn't just external distractions and interruptions that affect us. We have internal distractions that play an even bigger role in influencing the quality of our lives.

■ ■ ■

There are two phrases I've gotten a lot of mileage out of over the years joking around with my friends in the military and intelligence community. The first is "the engine is running but there's nobody behind the wheel" and its close cousin "the lights are on but nobody's home." The most generous meaning of these phrases is that they describe someone who is physically present but not really paying attention. On deployments and operational assignments, we used these phrases in much more derogatory ways to describe fellow soldiers or intelligence officers whose lack of situational awareness might get people killed because they weren't paying attention to what they were doing. The central theme remains constant—being somewhere or doing something physically but not being fully present mentally. Simplified further—physical presence without mental presence.

You know what I'm describing because you've been there before. Have you ever driven a car and somewhere along your journey you sort of "wake up" having missed a few miles (or more)? Perhaps you've driven through an intersection, then immediately hoped that the traffic light was green because you didn't even notice it. This happens to us all the time; our bodies are in one place but our minds are in another. We are often mentally time-traveling into the future, thinking about some event coming up, trying to predict it, being anxious about it, worried about it, or perhaps excited about it. When we aren't in the future, we are reliving the past, regretting something we've done, wishing we could change it, or holding on to something that's already gone. We do this so much that we barely notice what's happening right in front of us in the present moment. There are consequences to this.

According to research titled, "A Wandering Mind Is an Unhappy Mind," conducted in 2010 by a pair of Harvard psychologists, Matthew A. Killingsworth and Daniel T. Gilbert, our minds are wandering away from the present moment about 47% of the time.[16] The 2,250 people in the study were tracked via a phone application that enabled them to record their mood as well as the focus of their attention at random times throughout the day. As the data rolled in, the researchers began to piece together the impact of mind wandering on mood and general levels of happiness across a number of activities. They found that there was a positive correlation between mind wandering and unhappiness. Positive correlation in this case isn't actually a positive thing. What it means is that the more your mind wanders, the more likely you are to be unhappy.

People in the study reported significantly higher levels of happiness when they were focused in the present moment versus when their minds were wandering. The real kicker was that it didn't matter what activity they were doing. Let's take two fictional people in two very different situations and see what this means. Mike has been waiting in a very long TSA line and is situated directly behind a first-time flyer who doesn't know she needs to take off her shoes and belt or that she needs to take her laptop out of her bag and so she is delaying Mike even more. Maria is just resting in a chair at home. If Mike's attention is on the present moment and Maria's mind is wandering, it's more likely that Maria's mood will be less happy than Mike's. In fact, "resting" was one of the top-three activities people were least happy while doing it. The reason for that is quite simple. When you are resting, not really engaged in any particular activity, your mind wanders and, as the title of the study states, "a wandering mind is an unhappy mind."[17]

Physical presence without mental presence isn't just a recipe for getting yourself or others killed during high-risk operational situations or for cutting your hand while washing the dishes. We now know it's also a recipe for unhappiness. But why? I mean, isn't thinking good? Didn't thinking lead to all the amazing technologies and innovations I mentioned in our discussion on why companies carry out digital transformation? Artificial intelligence. Machine learning. Blockchain. Augmented reality. Didn't thinking lead to the development of many creature comforts such as air conditioning, DVRs, sliced bread, and pizza? Well, thinking did lead to the development of all those things but our thoughts aren't always very helpful.

● ● ●

Imagine, for a moment, your best friend. Whoever that is, bring them to mind as vividly as you can. And now, imagine your best friend says to you the things you've said to yourself during your most self-critical moments.

- You share there is an opportunity to apply for a manager role on your team and your best friend says, "You think *you* are qualified? You can't even lead yourself; how are you going to lead others?"
- You share that you just turned your white clothes pink after accidentally washing them with a new red shirt and your best friend responds, "You're an idiot. How could you make such a stupid mistake?"
- Your best friend sees you in your bathing suit and says, "Are you ever going to work out? Your body is disgusting."
- The person you tried to talk to at the bar just turned and walked away and your best friend says, "Did you really expect that person would be attracted to someone like you?"
- You share your frustration regarding how little progress you are making learning the piano and your best friend says, "Stop trying; you're never going to get it."

Would you be friends with *anyone* who talked to you in that way? I know I wouldn't be friends with my inner critic. We often talk to ourselves in ways that if another person talked to us in a similar manner, we'd probably get into a fight. Not only do we talk to ourselves this way, we often believe it.

The inner critic or inner judge isn't only harshly berating you after you've done something imperfectly; it's also hurling barbs and being generally pessimistic during the lead-up to certain activities and when you're trying to make a decision. Precisely when we are about to make a bold move or take innovative step, our inner critic chimes in with all that could go wrong, how you aren't suitable for the task, or that the risk is too great. This plays out in a wide variety of situations in our lives. This inner critic is at work when we are thinking of asking someone on a date, working through whether we should ask for a pay raise, and, as you've already read, deciding whether or not to apply to Harvard.

In fact, you could ask yourself that question right now to see what comes up. Ask yourself, "Could I get into Harvard?" If you are like most people, your inner response to that question was probably something along the lines of "AYFKM?" or "Hell, no!" If that is what your response was, you might say to me, "Well, of course, I'm going to think that; I'm not like the folks who get into Harvard. Folks who think to go to Harvard are super-confident and smart and probably wouldn't have that response." I thought that, too. Then, during orientation day for my graduate program at the Harvard Kennedy School, one of the administrators says to the crowd of us gathered in the Forum,[18] "There might be one person in this room, maybe two, who didn't think they could get into Harvard and when they received their acceptance letter they thought it could be a mix-up." Everyone laughed. Every single person. Why? Because the reality is, no one thinks he or she can get into Harvard. Most people just rule themselves out and don't apply, guaranteeing they won't get in. Then there are those who also don't think they can get in but apply anyway.

Here, again, a reasonable pushback from you might be, "Well, Harvard's acceptance rate is very low so it makes sense that people would automatically assume they can't get in." Automatically assuming anything is a pretty bad idea in most situations, but it runs much deeper. It would be one thing if people were only ruling themselves out of very low probability things such as winning the lottery, winning the Super Bowl, winning a gold medal in the Olympics, or taking a trip to the International Space Station. Unfortunately, it's not just considering low probability outcomes that triggers these types of thoughts. They occur when people begin to consider whether they could write a book, take a leadership position, start a business, sing karaoke, or speak in front of a crowd. There is a reason for this. We have this thing called a negativity bias and it wreaks havoc on our lives.

■ ■ ■

Imagine you're walking a narrow trail through a national park at dusk and suddenly you see a snake coiled on the path directly ahead.

A rush of adrenalin and fear wash over you and immediately stop you in your tracks. You glance to the left and right to see if there is a way around but the woods are darker now and so going around is not an option. You decide to walk the long way back to your camp-site and avoid the danger. The next day you walk the trail again and in the area where you saw the "snake" the night before, lay a coiled rope another hiker must have mistakenly dropped. You mistook the rope for a snake and avoided that route and that "danger," but there was no real danger. There are a number of lessons in this story and it is often told in Hindu and Buddhist contexts to convey concepts about seeing the true nature of reality. My use of it here is more Darwinian.

You see, it's very advantageous for us, from an evolutionary perspective, to see a rope on the ground and mistake it for a snake and then take steps to avoid it. It's much better to make *that* mistake than it is to make the opposite mistake. That is, seeing a snake on the ground and mistakenly thinking it's that rope you've been look-ing for all afternoon. You bend over to pick it up and suddenly you have a snake connected to your throat! Game over. Our ancestors who made that mistake, they didn't make it! We aren't related to them. We're related to those ancestors who made the first mistake and what we inherited from them was a tendency to see a threat where there is no threat, or if there is a threat, our brains amplify it so we'll make the safest choice, the choice that keeps us warm and snuggly in our comfort zone, and we already know what happens in our comfort zone.

As I mentioned, from an evolutionary perspective, this tendency of mind has been very helpful. What makes it a problem today is that we react to many non-life-threatening situations the same way we reacted 10,000 years ago when facing a potential saber-toothed tiger hidden in the rustling brush. It's not so helpful in the modern world when the "tiger" we are reacting to is the fear of public speak-ing, fear of criticism, fear of embarrassment, and fear of failure. We even react this way when merely facing a situation that isn't meeting our expectations.

Negativity bias basically colors our entire reality. It creates stories that aren't in service to our goals or our happiness and it can make rather benign situations seem miserable. Summarizing part of a joke by Louis C.K. here, it's why people, in a metal tube, going from New York to LA in 5 hours, experiencing the miracle of flight, will com-plain because the Wi-Fi is a little slow or because they had to wait

15 minutes on the taxiway.[19] I've seen grown men lash out at people seated near them on a plane because they weren't able to put their carry-on luggage in the overhead bin directly above their seat. What's happening here is that these folks are caught up noticing only what's not meeting their expectations and not noticing what's amazing right in front of them.

I'll grant you that the Wi-Fi is a bit slow on airplanes but it's sending an invisible signal to a satellite that humans built, put on top of a rocket, and launched into space and now it's orbiting our planet and connecting you to the largest volume of information ever collected in the history of humanity. That's kind of neat. You're also taking a trip in 5 hours that used to take 4 to 6 months and you had to take the trip with dozens of other people because the journey was so arduous that many people perished along the way.[20] So, it's pretty cool we can traverse the entire land mass of the United States in what is the equivalent of an afternoon and not have to resort to cannibalism.[21]

I don't want you to get the wrong impression here. Mindfulness isn't about putting blinders on or sweeping all negative experiences and situations under the rug and only seeing the positive or rainbows all the time, only having happy and joyful thoughts, and being blissed out. If you come across a teacher pushing that narrative, run away as quickly as you can because that person is sending you down a very unhelpful path. Mindfulness isn't about getting you into a particular state; it's a way to be fully awake and aware to meet any situation you happen to be in at the moment. One of the things mindfulness gives you is fuller access to the entire range of your experience. When you have access to the entire range of your experience instead of getting fixated only on what isn't meeting your expectations, your experience of life changes.

■ ■ ■

We've spent some time in this chapter talking about why you might want to consider picking up a mindfulness practice. The world has changed from analog to digital. The demands on our time and attention have increased dramatically and our go-to method to meet the higher demand—multitasking—is actually inefficient and increases our stress and anxiety. We are bombarded by distractions nearly all our waking hours, our minds are wandering about 47% of the time, and we're fixated on the negative. This is making us unhappy even when things are about as good as they can get from a historical perspective, in terms of wealth, health care, and quality of life. This is a situation negatively affecting hundreds of millions of people, and when that happens, scientists begin looking at methods or interventions that claim to address these challenges. Many make this claim about mindfulness, so let's see what scientists say about why mindfulness might be beneficial in the modern world.

Chapter 3

(Some of) The Science of Mindfulness

One thing I have discovered over the years delivering keynotes and training on mindfulness around the world is that some people want to make sure someone in a white lab coat has confirmed the validity of mindfulness before they will try it. It's not that they are singling out mindfulness; whether it is a specific diet plan, an exercise regime, or a mindfulness practice, some people just want to know the science before they will make the investment in time and effort. I can understand that position in today's busy world with marketers constantly trying to get you to do the latest amazing thing that is going to solve all your problems. Also, I personally love science and enjoy reading the latest studies on a number of topics, but what's more compelling to me regarding the decision to add a new practice to my life is whether or not it has withstood the test of time. Mindfulness, across all the contemplative traditions that have used it, certainly meets that criterion. Additionally, having sat through statistics classes at Harvard and seeing how easily they can be manipulated, learning about practices such as "p-hacking,"[1] used to manipulate research findings, and reading about the replication crisis in social science and psychology research, I never automatically take research at face value these days. I'm inclined to try things myself and see if they work for me. Trust but verify.

There have been entire books diving deep into the tens of thousands of scientific research studies on mindfulness written by mindfulness researchers for other mindfulness researchers. This is not that book and I am not a scientist. We are just going to dip our toe into the science. I offer this brief look at some of the research findings regarding mindfulness but strongly suggest that the most important factor you should weigh is the impact of a consistent mindfulness practice on your life and those around you. There have been millions of people who have come before us on a mindfulness journey, and most came well before modern scientists ever cared about what it did to the brain. In my opinion, the science is finally catching up with what countless others have known for millennia: what you do with your mind matters. What I will try to do in the pages that follow is share with you, in a general way, with as little technical jargon as possible, some of the research I found compelling as well as research that aligns with my personal experience with mindfulness. I will also share a couple recommendations of books to consider reading if you want to take a deeper dive into the science.

Mindfulness Changes the Brain

I hate to burst the bubble here but this has to be done. There are dozens if not hundreds of news articles, magazine covers, podcasts, and mindfulness teachers that effusively tout the fact that mindfulness changes the brain[2] as if this is the crucial scientific finding that should convince you to start a mindfulness practice immediately. They are not wrong in their conviction that mindfulness changes the brain; it most certainly does. What they fail to tell you or what they do not know themselves is that pretty much everything changes the brain. Begin learning to play the piano and the brain changes. Start a new workout and the brain changes. Read a book and the brain changes. (Yes, your brain has changed because you are reading this book. You're welcome.) Notice there is a loose tile on the bathroom floor you've been using on a near daily basis for the last 10 years and, even then, the brain changes.

Your brain changes all the time, and this ability of your brain to change is called neuroplasticity. What's special about mindfulness is that it changes the brain in ways that seem to correlate with changes in behavior, perception, and experience that have benefits not only for the mindfulness practitioner but also for those around them. Let's look at some of the changes uncovered by putting meditators and non-meditators into brain scanners before, during, and after mindfulness training.

Mindfulness Reduces the Size and Activity in the Amygdala

The amygdala is kind of like a guard. It is designed to alert us and protect us from danger (among many other functions). It is where the flight, fight, or freeze automatic reaction comes from when we detect a threat in our environment. It's highly reactive and does not consider consequences. It is focused on survival and therefore diligently pulls our attention to anything that might be a threat. When that happens, it sets off an internal process leading to the immediate release of cortisol, commonly referred to as the stress hormone, and other hormones to prepare us for action to protect ourselves. As I mentioned, these types of functions of our brain were (and are still in some cases) extremely valuable when we were facing saber-toothed tigers or other such threats. It's not that the amygdala is bad in and of itself. It's that the automatic survival reaction is often triggered by our most common modern-day "threats," such as criticism, failure, public speaking, and other things that are not actually threats to our lives.

The reduction in the size and activity of the amygdala seems to correlate with less anxious and fewer reactive behaviors in the real world.[3] I can attest that in my life, since I've been meditating more diligently, I am much less reactive when things don't go my way, when someone does or says something upsetting, or when my son does not listen after the eighth time asking him to pick up his toys. It's not that I never react or say something I later regret, but it happens much less today than it did before meditating daily. The benefits of being able to respond to those situations versus reacting out of frustration, pain, or anger cannot be overstated. What situations in your life would be better handled with a thoughtful response as opposed to an automatic reaction?

Mindfulness Increases Activity in the Anterior Cingulate Cortex (ACC)

You might think of the ACC as your wise advisor. This part of the brain is associated with thoughtful decisions, self-control (as opposed to impulsive/compulsive behavior), and emotional regulation. Imagine you are someone who craves and indulges in smoking, porn, video games, snacks, social media, or reality TV from time to time. Perhaps you would like to do/use less of those things but somehow you find yourself indulging in them a bit more than you'd like. Carrying out mindfulness exercises seems to provide some help here. The ACC is a key player in our ability to manage our impulses and cravings. What the science suggests is that more activity in this region of the brain is correlated with reduced cravings and an increased ability to manage our emotions.[4] I don't know about you, but I cannot see any downsides to an outcome like that.

When I was in my early 20s, I was that guy who spent too much time in the virtual world as opposed to the real world, wanting to get online immediately after waking up or after work and connect with my "friends." My "drug" of choice was a game called EverQuest or, as I came to call it, "Evercrack." It was a very successful massively multiplayer online role-playing game that required a great deal of time and attention to successfully increase one's level and status in the game. I probably played that game on a near daily basis for a year and finally had to quit cold turkey after my lack of attention elsewhere damaged an important relationship. In the years that followed, I deliberately avoided all video games out of fear I would get addicted if I played even once. Fast forward more than two decades later and a daily mindfulness practice, I finally allowed a video game console in my house, initially for my nieces and nephews, but now for my son who loves Minecraft. I play the game with him from time to time and have not had anything near the type of craving I had in the past. It could just be maturity or a shift in priorities. However, I suspect the real change is more my ability to see an impulse arise in the moment and not get carried away or caught, and I attribute that to my mindfulness practice.

Mindfulness Increases the Size of Your Hippocampus

Your hippocampus is kind of like a flash or USB drive; some of its key functions are related to moving short-term memory into long-term memory, working memory, spatial memory, and other memory-related functions. Numerous studies show mindfulness practice correlates with increases in the size of the hippocampus,[5] increases in working memory,[6] and decreases in older memories interfering with the acquisition of newer memories, a phenomenon known as "proactive interference." Researchers believe mindfulness exercises may be responsible for reducing or slowing negative impacts on memory function due to aging, PTSD, and depression.

For those of you thinking of going to graduate school someday, in addition to the working memory increases and other memory-related benefits, mindfulness was shown to increase Graduate Record Examinations (GRE) scores. A quote from one study's abstract said

> Mindfulness training improved both GRE reading-comprehension scores and working memory capacity while simultaneously reducing the occurrence of distracting thoughts during completion of the GRE and the measure of working memory. Improvements in performance following mindfulness training were mediated by reduced mind wandering among participants who were prone to distraction at pretesting. Our results suggest that cultivating mindfulness is an effective and efficient technique for improving cognitive function, with wide-reaching consequences.[7]

I cannot remember if mindfulness has helped my memory but I do know it has helped my marriage; I've not forgotten any of my wedding anniversaries or my wife's birthday in the time we have been together. I've heard the best way to remember your anniversary is to forget it once and so I'm putting a flag in the ground for the second-best way: practice mindfulness. It's definitely much less painful than forgetting an anniversary.

Mindfulness Increases the Size of Your Insula

Your insula could be considered your sage or saintly self. It has been associated with our experience of compassion, empathy, love, and other emotions, as well as awareness of bodily sensations and our perception of self. When you feel deeply connected to or in love with someone, your insula is helping you experience those emotions. This is pretty important stuff when it comes to connection and relationships, but why would noticing bodily sensations make any difference in our ability to connect with others or maintain relationships?

Sensations are the fundamental building blocks of our experience of emotion. Think about the last time you were suddenly asked to speak to a group of people without warning or to come to the front of the room to introduce yourself to a group of people you've just met. Situations like that tend to result in a somewhat queasy feeling in the pit of our stomachs, which we might label anxiety. Can you remember the last time you were surprised or scared? What did it feel like in the body? Sudden tingling in your chest and a racing heart? Have you ever felt the heat of embarrassment as your face flushes red with blood? It's our physiological sensations that, in a certain configuration or signature, get labeled "love," "anger," "frustration," "joy," and all the other variations of emotions you experience on a daily basis. Your signatures are different than mine. Mindfulness practice seems to strengthen the insula's ability to give us clearer perception of these sensations,[8] which can help us notice and name our emotions earlier. What do you think noticing anger arising 30 seconds earlier than you currently do would enable you to do in the middle of a disagreement? Could it give you extra time to respond versus react?

Not only do you gain improved levels of self-awareness through mindfulness meditation, research also suggests changes in insula through mindfulness practice correlate to a greater ability to "feel" another person's pain or distress, which may spur a more compassionate response.[9] You know yourself better and you know others better. That's a recipe for relationship success. The ability to respond to heated situations with poise while also exhibiting greater compassion seems quite saintly to me.

Similar to the other discussed areas of the brain, the insula seems to be associated with a number of functions beyond what I list here, but for our purposes this is enough to get a sense of some impacts mindfulness seems to have on this very important part of the brain.

■ ■ ■

According to the American Mindfulness Research Association there were over 1,200 mindfulness journal articles published in 2019 alone.[10] I have only barely scratched the surface regarding the research pointing to the benefits of mindfulness practice. However, just as you do not need to know all of the physics and engineering of the internal combustion engine to benefit from having one in your car, you also do not need to understand all the underlying brain processes affected by mindfulness to benefit from practicing it. Even if a scientist or meditator understood all the neural correlates of attention (no one does), she would not automatically be able to control her attention any better than you. It takes much more than intellectual understanding to affect what our minds habitually do; it takes consistent practice.

If you want to dive deeper into the research into mindfulness, I suggest a number of books in the notes section for this chapter,[11] but I want you to walk away from this chapter with more than just some intellectual understanding of how the brain changes in response to mindfulness. I want you to walk away inspired to start practicing!

The changes in the brain I have described in this chapter seem to cultivate an improved ability to recognize when we are (or about to be) in the fight, flight, or freeze automatic survival reaction mode, enabling us to shift into meeting our circumstances from a place of thoughtful response. The changes also seem to help make us more aware of ourselves, our surroundings, and our unhelpful impulses, giving us precious time to intervene to make wiser choices rather than noticing only after we have said or done something we regret. How would those new responses to life affect you and those around you? How would being able to respond thoughtfully in the middle of a crisis affect your ability to inspire confidence in those you lead or who look up to you? Let's put the science aside for now and see how our brains work in the real world without mindfulness.

Chapter 4

How Do Our Brains Work outside a Brain Scanner?

As wonderful as science is, the descriptions of findings in research papers typically fail to illustrate the practical value in any meaningful or memorable way for the layperson. It is not that researchers are incapable in this respect, it's more that these papers are written by researchers for researchers, in the hopes that they expand the bounds of human knowledge on the subject and to do that they have to speak in very precise scientific terms that don't always easily translate to real-world descriptions. So, let's go through some real-life examples of common situations you might find yourself in from time to time and see how your brain reacts.

I'm going to take you through two scenarios. What I'd like you to do is put yourself into the scenario, mentally visualize it as vividly as you can, and notice what emotions, thoughts, and impulses come up for you in reaction to what is happening in the scenario. If you have a piece of paper handy, it might be helpful to note down your reaction to each question before moving to the next page.

Scenario one. You are on your morning drive to work and traffic is moderately heavy. As you approach your exit from the highway, a silver Mercedes SUV zooms ahead on your left-hand side and quickly pulls into the exit lane directly in front of you.

1. What emotions came up?
2. What thoughts did you have?
3. What impulses to action did you have?

Scenario two. You are walking down a hallway at work. You see a colleague up ahead walking toward you. As you approach, you make direct eye contact, wave, and say, "hi." However, your colleague walks by and doesn't acknowledge you at all.

1. What emotions came up?
2. What thoughts did you have?
3. What impulses to action did you have?

When I share these exercises in workshops, courses, or keynotes, I get startlingly similar results. Perhaps these will ring true for you. Let's first take a look at the most common answers to the questions in scenario one, the zooming driver.

1. What emotions come up?
   a. Anger, frustration, annoyance, rage, indignation
2. What thoughts do you have?
   a. "What a jerk!" "What a selfish person." "Oh, there goes someone who thinks he is more important than everyone else!" "Entitled dirtbag!"
3. What impulses to action do you have?
   a. "I would give a colorful hand gesture." "Wish I could give him a piece of my mind." "I would drive really close to his rear bumper so he's knows I'm upset." "Roll down my window and yell a few expletives."

Did these ring true in terms of your reaction to the scenario? Participants in my courses quickly, and nearly unanimously, conclude the zooming driver believes he is more important than others and is somewhat (or very) selfish. This practically universal reaction seems to further cement the accuracy of the judgment of the other driver's character. We are all feeling good now; we know a jerk when we see one and this guy takes the cake. Now let's take a look at the most common answers to the questions in scenario two, the nonresponsive colleague:

1. What emotions come up?
   a. Embarrassment, sadness, anger, annoyance, indifference, worry (self-focused), concern (other-focused)

2. What thoughts do you have?
   a. "I hope no one saw that." "No one likes me." "I'm invisible." "What a jerk!" "Well, I never!" "Whatever." "Did he even see me?" "What did I do to upset him?" "I hope he is okay."
3. What impulses to action do you have?
   a. "I'd just want to disappear." "I'd probably sit at my desk and wonder what I did to upset him." "I'd ignore him next time." "I'd stop talking to him." "I'd send him a note asking if I've done something to offend him." "I'd send him a note to make sure everything is okay."

In contrast to scenario one, the emotional reactions to scenario two are all over the map. We have one situation, but we have at least seven different emotional reactions. This happens every time I describe this scenario in a class. I hear everything from sadness to anger to indifference to embarrassment. One person reads or hears the scenario and is immediately mortified; he gets a sinking feeling in his stomach and wants to retreat to his cubicle. Another person is immediately annoyed and endeavors to "never talk to that jerk again!" What gives? How can there be such varying emotional responses to the exact same scenario and what does that say about what is causing our emotional reactions? In a word: meaning. In five words: the meaning you make up. In 18 words: the meaning you make up in your head automatically while being unaware that it is happening at all.

In the second scenario, to feel angry, you would have to believe some variation of "the person ignored me on purpose and possibly wants me to feel bad." Which brings up another aspect of this automatic assessment process: ascribing intent to others' actions. We often automatically assume intent based on the emotion we feel. You only need to consider scenario one to see this in action; virtually everyone assumes ill intent on the part of the driver because we feel anger, rage, or annoyance and we have absolutely no idea why that person got in front of us in the exit lane. If you knew the driver was trying to get to the hospital to see his dying mother, your anger would evaporate almost immediately. Similarly, if you feel bad in reaction to a comment from your partner, you likely automatically assume your partner intended to make you feel bad and respond accordingly. All of this automaticity leads to inaccurate assumptions, assessments, and appraisals that go unchecked and negatively affect personal and professional relationships alike. We can assume ourselves into bad relationships that otherwise would be fine without all the assumptions.

We are meaning-making machines. As a situation unfolds, your brain automatically appraises it and assigns meaning to what just happened, and it does so from a very limited point of view: yours. Once the meaning is accepted, which also happens automatically and unconsciously in the *untrained* mind, your emotional response arises. When that happens, it's all over (for most people), because confirmation bias kicks in, which leads the subsequent thoughts, judgments, and impulses to be in alignment with the accepted meaning because the brain deletes, distorts, and overlooks information in contravention to the accepted meaning. Now all future interactions with the person who walked by you and didn't acknowledge your hello will be seen through the lens of all this meaning you automatically made up. You'll begin to primarily notice behaviors that reinforce your earlier assessment and you will be much less likely to register behaviors that contradict it. This is why first impressions are so important; they tend to stick regardless of the behavior that comes after. By the way, "impression" is just another word for meaning that is equally automatically made up on the fly.

You might chafe at this and say, "It's context dependent and I would likely have a history with the person who walked by which would make my reaction accurate." We all like to believe our automatic reactions and assumptions are accurate, and I admit your reactions are probably accurate some of the time, but let's just look at what happened in scenario two. Did you have an emotional reaction? Any emotional reaction at all? Be honest. Everyone in my classes has some kind of emotional reaction to the scenario in which someone walks by and does not acknowledge that person. Now notice, I did not identify any particular person other than "colleague," nor did I provide any information as to why that person didn't acknowledge you as he or she walked by you in the hallway and yet you had your personal reaction to the situation. Maybe the person did not see you. Maybe the person was lost in thought. Maybe the person was in a rush and had to use the bathroom. Maybe the person doesn't like you. Maybe the person is annoyed with you because of something you said in a meeting that was upsetting. I'll bet if we had an extremely long hallway and that person was lost in thought not acknowledging anyone saying "hi" we'd have the same situation: dozens of people having their own personal reaction based on the meaning they just made up in their heads.

Furthermore, let's look at scenario one. I did not say the driver was speeding, did not say he cut you off when merging into the exit lane, and did not say anything about his character. Yet, if you are similar to the vast majority of people who read/hear that scenario, you had a reaction similar to those I shared from my classes. All of those very pertinent details were left out. This was a hypothetical situation, and yet your brain automatically filled in the gaps and you had an emotional reaction. Any emotional reaction you had came from you; it was born out of the meaning you assigned to that behavior, action, and situation and it had no basis in reality at all. There was no reality; it was a made-up exercise. These automatic mental processes are where unconscious bias rears its head. They are what keep us in cycles of conflict with others, and they lead us into many preventable misunderstandings.

It's important to note that you are not doing this deliberately; this is happening automatically and, for the vast majority of people, unconsciously. This does not make you a bad person. These automatic assessments and appraisals are influenced by a dizzying array of things such as our beliefs, values, societal norms, past experiences, mood, or even whether we are hungry, angry, lonely, or tired.

So what do we do about it? This book isn't called *Mindfulness without the Bells and Beads* for nothing. We will soon practice something called "focused attention meditation," so we can cultivate the focus and concentration required to notice what we do with our own minds, which leads to the wisdom required to step out of those unhelpful thought streams, or as I like to call it: Catch and Release! A consistent mindfulness practice helps create the clarity needed to get inside the gears of this automatic process and habit of mind and enables you to become aware of it. Once you are aware of something, you can do something about it.

A mindfulness practice is not going to prevent that automatic meaning making from occurring but as you continue to practice you will begin to "catch" this process happening. After mindfulness practice for a couple weeks, maybe you realize that you made some unfounded assumptions about your partner's intent but you didn't realize it until 45 minutes after an argument. Now you can deliberately take another perspective and, perhaps more important, check in with you partner on your assumptions. After more practice maybe you realize you did it and it was only 20 minutes after the interaction occurred, then 10 minutes after, then 5, and at some point, you'll Catch that automatic appraisal with all its attendant assumptions, arise in the moment, and be able to Release the impulse to react and instead respond mindfully. Whether it's leading your team or organization in the midst of a crisis or navigating a heated disagreement with your spouse, being able to respond is always better than automatically reacting. This is what all those studies I referenced in Chapter 3 seem to show: a consistent mindfulness meditation practice changes in the brain in ways that seem to correlate with a greater ability to respond to life thoughtfully versus react automatically.

■ ■ ■

At this point, you might be asking, "Because I don't yet have a consistent mindfulness practice, is there anything I can begin to do today to reduce the likelihood of reacting in a way I later regret?" Yes, there is. In addition to the formal mindfulness meditation practices you'll learn shortly, there are informal practices that can be brought to bear in the moment to help manage situations. A formal practice is one that you set aside time to do, for example, spending 15 minutes in the morning to do an awareness-of-breath meditation (which I'll cover shortly.) An informal practice is one that you can do throughout your day. These are things such as mindfully brushing your teeth by intentionally tuning into all the sensations of that action, such as deliberately noticing how the bristles feel on your gums, the taste of the toothpaste, the feeling of the toothbrush in your hand, and so on. Other in-the-moment, informal practices are designed to help us navigate challenging situations or provide us a small space from which to move into our next moment intentionally. One particularly useful informal practice is called the S.T.O.P. practice. Until Catch and Release became second nature for me, I used the S.T.O.P. practice in between the Catching of an unhelpful thought, story, or belief and the Releasing of it. You can use this Catch—S.T.O.P—and Release technique in the midst of a discussion that is becoming heated and you want to increase the odds that you will respond instead of react automatically. The S.T.O.P. practice by itself can also be used between meetings just to reset before moving into another meeting. Once you are familiar with this practice you can do it in just a few seconds anytime it is needed. I adapted my version of the exercise from the S.T.O.P. practice noted in Elisha Goldstein's book, *The Now Effect: How This Moment Can Change the Rest of Your Life*.[1] S.T.O.P. is an acronym for Stop, Take a breath, Observe, and Pose and Proceed. I added Pose to my version of S.T.O.P.

S—Stop. Pause and stop all activity for just a moment or two.

T—Take a breath. Take a breath and notice the sensations of breathing. Perhaps you notice cool air coming in your nose and warm air coming out. Taking a deep breath is optional.

O—Observe. Notice something in your external environment. Perhaps notice the pattern in the carpet, items on your desk, pictures or paintings on the wall. Then turn that focus inward and notice what's happening inside you. What thoughts, feelings, and emotions are present? Don't try to push them away or suppress them but instead acknowledge their presence.

P—Pose and Proceed. Pose the question to yourself silently, "What's important now?" Then allow, if you can, what comes up in response to that question to inform your intention for the next moment of your day.

One situation in which I consistently use this practice is when I've parked my car at home after a long day at the office. I go through each step of the practice and when I get to Pose and Proceed, typically for me, at that moment of the day, the response to "What's important now?" is that I want to walk into my house and be as present as possible for my wife and 5-year-old son. Then I gather my things and walk into the house. Does that mean that during the entire evening I never get on my phone to check work email or pull up social media? No, that's not very realistic in today's culture. Plus, I'm in the working world and sometimes there is very good reason to check work email at home. The evening is also when I get on social media to write and read posts. However, if I don't do this practice, I am much more likely to reach for my phone out of sheer habit even if it is not ringing, pinging, or vibrating. When that happens, we often become oblivious to the world around us.

My 5-year old son routinely wants to tell me stories about things he learned at school or about his latest bug discovery in our backyard. If I try to multitask with my phone during that "conversation," it is quite likely that he will just stop telling me the story in the middle of it and walk away because he knows I'm not paying attention. That interaction will stick in his young mind and inform his thoughts about how important he is to me. How do you feel when you know someone is not paying attention to you? Is it a good feeling? As slick as you think you are, others, especially children, can tell when you are looking at your phone in your lap, at the side of your leg, or wherever else you try to hide (or not hide) it while pretending to pay attention. Pretending to pay attention is essentially pretending someone is important to you when, clearly, that person is not. On my side, I might not even register that my son stopped the conversation midway through due to me being so engrossed in my phone. Over time he'll just stop sharing those stories and stop wanting to initiate conversations with me because, despite what I say, he will have the direct experience of what I actually do. Even 5-year-old children know that actions trump words every time. That's not an experience I'm keen to be responsible for giving my son or my wife.

■ ■ ■

These are some of the most meaningful elements of mindfulness that the scientific findings fail to convey when they describe changes in the brain such as reduced size and activity in the amygdala or increased cortical volume of the insula. The descriptions of all those neurological changes are extremely important but pale in comparison to the actual impact formal and informal mindfulness practices have on one's relationships, career, and personal life.

When you can Catch unhelpful stories, beliefs, thoughts, and judgments and Release them and the tendency to react automatically, your ability to lead, perform, and take care of yourself and your loved ones improves dramatically.

Now that the stage has been set, let's dive into what mindfulness really is.

Chapter 5

Finding the Signal in the Mindfulness Noise

It's clear to anyone who has picked up a magazine or newspaper or has perused any social media feed in the last 5 years that mindfulness is hot right now, and I must admit, it is one of the reasons why I got the deal to write this book. Just searching the term "mindfulness" on Google yields 264 million results![1] Unfortunately, many of the items the search results point to aren't actually mindfulness related practices. Many results are the outcome of savvy marketing and search engine optimization to get you to buy a product or sometimes even to buy into a worldview.

It's staggering seeing so many products, activities, exercises, social movements, and meditation techniques in the world today that just 15 to 20 years ago didn't carry the mindfulness moniker alongside them but now seem determined to prove they were in the mindfulness camp all along. Executive presence courses have become executive presence and mindfulness courses. Yogic breathing exercises are now passed off as mindfulness exercises. Yoga teachers claim to be mindfulness teachers. Plain old mayonnaise has become mindful mayonnaise. Money and attention tend to lead to this style of marketing or "we've always been *xyz*" type claims but with something as impactful as mindfulness can be, it is quite counterproductive because people looking for the benefits of mindfulness may not be learning actual mindfulness practices. If you want to reap the benefits of mindfulness, it behooves you to do genuine mindfulness practices.

I spend a great deal of time on the road delivering keynotes, workshops, and other training to a variety of clients interested in mindfulness. These events are often held in large hotels, sprawling conference centers, or the occasional private villa in an exclusive resort catering to high-net-worth individuals or c-suite executives. There are often multiple corporate events running concurrently at these venues, and as I've roamed around them, I've had the opportunity to step into a few other "mindfulness" sessions (which are now a part of many large corporate events).

I'm sad to report it seems as if any exercise that involves closing one's eyes or breathing can be passed off as mindfulness and because most people do not know what it really is, the person in the front of the room can say (or sell) whatever he or she wants with impunity.

Following are some examples of event titles I've seen at different corporate events or have seen on event materials and agendas claiming to be mindfulness in their titles or descriptions:

"Mindfulness Session: Laughing Yoga"
"Today's Mindfulness Class—Yogic Breathing"
"Learning from Near-Death Experiences"
"Mindful Social Action"
"Floating Yoga"
"Connecting with Crystals"
"Sound Bathing"
"Guided Visualizations for Relaxation"

It might be surprising to you, given all the deliberate conflation of mindfulness with these types of activities that none of the aforementioned is actually mindfulness.

It's not just the purveyors of various non-mindfulness-related techniques, perspectives, and exercises that slap on the mindfulness label to get in on the action or to co-op the mindfulness movement for their own purposes; it's also consumer products. Take 5 minutes to do a basic internet search on mindful products and you'll not only find mindful mayonnaise as mentioned but also mindful pistachio nuts, mindful skin cream, mindful salt, mindful soap, mindful tea, mindful essential oils, and, of course, mindful coloring books.

Let me make a quick disclaimer here. I'm not saying any of those activities, exercises, products, and so on are bad or that they are not beneficial in some or even many ways. I'm merely saying they are not mindfulness. So, the question that might be arising in your mind right now is, "If none of these things is mindfulness, what actually *is* mindfulness?" Well, I'm glad you asked, and we'll get to that in a moment, but there is another source of noise surrounding mindfulness that inadvertently serves to alienate millions of people who could benefit from these practices: all the unnecessary accessories, such as bells, beads, and Buddhist beliefs.

■ ■ ■

On February 23, 1993, the PBS documentary series Healing the Mind with Bill Moyers aired an episode entitled "Healing from Within."[2] This episode featured Jon Kabat-Zinn, the creator of the popular Mindfulness-Based Stress Reduction (MBSR) course, who is credited with bringing secular mindfulness into the mainstream. The episode catapulted Zinn's reach and since that time has enabled him to make mindfulness a common term around the world. Zinn's MBSR program is so well regarded and its positive impacts on participants are so well documented that it is essentially the bar by which all other mindfulness-based interventions are measured. (Full disclosure: I'm an MBSR teacher.) Yet, even in this secular course, as aired in the Healing the Mind series, there are people sitting in half-lotus position on special meditation cushions called zafus and Zinn using Tibetan cymbals to start and finish his guided meditations.

Fast-forward to present day and MBSR courses as well as most other mindfulness courses, including those apparently tailored for corporate audiences, still continue to be taught in this way, with the ringing of bells and/or the dolling out of special meditation cushions in class. Many mindfulness teachers show up with Buddhist beads around their necks or wrists, carrying their own tiny bell, and sometimes bringing along a small flower to sit beside them as they teach (a common prop in many Buddhist, Hindu, and Advaita Vendānta religious teaching sessions) and so it's no wonder why some teachers may have a difficult time reaching the corporate world. I don't agree with recent criticisms that MBSR and other secular mindfulness-based training programs are just sneaky ways to spread Buddhism, but this way of teaching hardly strikes a secular tone.

App-based meditation training is often no better. Don't get me wrong. There are very good apps out there and I use them in my courses but much of their content carries the same sheen of spirituality and new age sentiment. In some apps, it can be difficult to find meditations that are not deliberately guided in sickly sweet tones, with words uttered breathlessly, or with commentary such as, "You are a universal being whose heart coherence can be shaped to connect with the one and only true source of love which abounds all sacred life." I do not think there is a more effective way of alienating non-spiritual/nonreligious people and pushing them *away* from building mindfulness skills than the current way mindfulness is most often framed, promoted, and taught.

Let me set the record straight. Although many mindfulness teachers and practitioners are attached to the things on the following list and other things you probably associate with meditation, you do not need any of them to authentically practice and reap the benefits of mindfulness. Furthermore, none of these will make you "better" at cultivating mindfulness.

◆ Bells
◆ Beads
◆ Bracelets
◆ Buddhist or other religious beliefs
◆ Tibetan cymbals
◆ Robes
◆ A special meditation cushion
◆ Incense
◆ Candles
◆ A yoga mat
◆ A yoga studio membership
◆ A trip to India
◆ A toe ring
◆ A tattoo of the Hindu mantra "om mani padme hum"
◆ A tattoo of any of the Chinese characters for peace, openness, mindfulness, oneness, strength, or presence
◆ A "Zen nook" or meditation room in your apartment
◆ "Singing" bowls
◆ A tiny statue of the Buddha
◆ A tiny statue of Ganesha, Shiva, Vishnu, or other Hindu deities
◆ Really long flowing pants, skirts, or scarves

These things are like pearls, quite beautiful in some respects and wearing them helps people project a certain image to others, which is extremely important to many. However, that outer sparkle distracts from the true core without which there would be no pearl. With mindfulness, far too many get ensnared by and attached to the outer shell, the pretty accessories that project they are mindful people, and completely miss the true essence. It's not that there is anything inherently wrong with the things on this list. Some, like a tiny statue of the Buddha, could serve as a cue to remind you to do a mindfulness practice but so could a yellow sticky note on your bathroom mirror and that's my point here. The bottom line is that you don't need to add any of these things to your life to practice mindfulness effectively, and in fact getting attached to them can be a real hindrance to your practice. So, if you don't like the things on that list or have been averse to learning more about mindfulness because you thought you would need to buy them or buy into new age spirituality, worry no more. You can save your money. Not having them won't prevent you from learning and benefiting from mindfulness.

What do you need to begin to practice and reap the benefits of mindfulness? Just five things:

1. Be alive and conscious.
2. Have a place to stand, sit, walk, or lie down.
3. Have a basic understanding of what mindfulness is and isn't.
4. Know which practices actually cultivate mindfulness.
5. Have a commitment to practicing regularly, preferably daily.

Now, let's start to work on number 3 and find the signal in the noise.

■ ■ ■

Understanding what mindfulness is can be a challenge when its meaning is obfuscated by all the hype. Also, who wants to sift through 264 million internet search results when many of them are twisted to encompass things clearly *not* mindfulness? So, let's start with a simple definition. At a basic level:

Mindfulness is an ability to keep attention on one's present moment experience without getting too caught up in automatic thoughts and judgments.

That's it. That's the kernel so many other activities, approaches, and attitudes layer over and obscure.

. . .

A small aside before we dive a little deeper. I said in the Introduction I would keep this book practical and that I was not going to be delivering an academic research style treatise on the origins of mindfulness. I'm sticking to that commitment but also have to acknowledge there are other opinions and definitions of mindfulness out there. My definition is adapted from Jon Kabat-Zinn's version from his bestselling book, *Wherever You Go, There You Are*, where he writes, "Mindfulness means paying attention in a particular way: on purpose, in the present moment, and nonjudgmentally."[3] Zinn's definition is the most widely accepted secular definition of mindfulness but I've decided to break from it slightly due to my perspective on the nonjudgmental aspect of mindfulness, which I will discuss in Chapter 10. Also, if you get into an academic debate with researchers or religious scholars who have spent years poring over, translating, or diligently adhering to ancient Buddhist writings attributed to the historical Buddha such as the Dhammapada and Satipatthana Sutta, you'll hear various views and nuances. The Satipatthana Sutta is the primary source for Buddhism's definition of mindfulness. That said, as much as some people would like you to believe, Buddhism hasn't cornered the market on mindfulness. Various religions, secular philosophies, and other contemplative traditions have concepts strikingly similar to Buddhism's version of mindfulness. If you are interested in a quick read that describes the many ways mindfulness-style practices and approaches to learning how one's mind works and exercising it in a particular way show up in history under different names, I'd recommend *Stillness Is the Key: An Ancient Strategy for Modern Life* by Ryan Holiday.[4]

. . .

Now back to my definition of mindfulness. Here it is again for your convenience. Mindfulness is an ability to keep attention on one's present moment experience without getting too caught up in automatic thoughts and judgments. You may be thinking, "Okay, in English please." It's present moment awareness without getting caught up in your running commentary on the world. Allow me to elaborate by taking you on a short journey.

You've just stepped into the elevator at work and glance at your watch: 6:50 am. It's Monday morning and you have a 7:00 am meeting with your colleagues in the conference room of your office. Work typically starts at 9:00 so you woke up extra early and skipped making coffee and breakfast to get out the house quickly. You're not a morning person so skipping the coffee is kind of a risk but these meetings are always catered so you can count on a hot cup of coffee and those delectable croissants the boss's executive assistant always orders. Stepping off the elevator you can already smell the croissants. You walk down the hall and into the conference room. First person there. You beeline for the croissants and coffee and immediately notice there is no coffee. You think, "Oh, no, there's no coffee!" You quickly look around and confirm there is no coffee in the room (and you already know your office doesn't have coffee machines.) You glance at your watch; 6:55 am. There's no time to run down and get coffee. You think, "Well, isn't this just great. How am I going to get through this meeting? What a horrible morning and now I'm going to be tired and in a bad mood all day!"

Okay, let's look at what happened, particularly right near the end of that story. You walked into the conference room and could see with your own eyes there was no coffee and yet you said to yourself, "There's no coffee." Who were you talking to or informing there was no coffee? Yourself? That's the internal voice we have that accompanies and narrates most of our experiences.

Now that was a slightly negative experience: walking in and seeing there was no coffee is a coffee person's worst nightmare. It could have gone differently. Maybe you walk into the conference room and they have your favorite coffee, Starbucks or Dunkin' brand. As soon as you recognize your favorite coffee you say to yourself, "Wow, it's my favorite coffee! What an awesome surprise and wonderful way to start the meeting. I'm going to have such a great day today! I work for such a great company!" A bit of hyperbole here for effect but you get the point. Again, you can see with your own eyes it is your favorite coffee and yet some part of your brain narrates that experience. That is the inner voice again. Also, in addition to judging and narrating the experience in real time, did you notice how quickly the mind slipped into pre-living the future and predicting how the rest of the day was going to go based on one small thing that did not meet (or exceeded) your expectations? This is what the mind does nearly every waking moment whether we are aware of it or not, and that inner dialogue has a massive impact on our behavior, well-being, performance, and experience of the world.

The signal in all the mindfulness noise is this. The initial aim of mindfulness practice is to increase our ability to turn toward and be fully engaged with our present moment experience, no matter what it is, and to become more aware of and unshackle ourselves from the mind's incessant judgment, which lessens its impact on our state of being and reduces our habitual reactivity to life. When cultivated, mindfulness enables us to meet life in its totality, including the ups and downs, with openness and broader perspective, allowing us to respond more creatively and less bound by past patterns, limiting beliefs, and the stories we tell ourselves. Are you ready to start?

Chapter 6

The Fundamentals of Cultivating Mindfulness

The first step in understanding how to cultivate mindfulness requires knowing what exercises genuinely lead to the improvement of this skill. Unfortunately, due to mindfulness's current status as something all purveyors of self-development training want to highlight their program develops, this, too, is a cloudy notion when trying to find ground truth. Let's start with a fundamental distinction: the relationship between mindfulness and meditation. These two terms are so often conflated and used interchangeably that many people, including "teachers" who purport to be teaching mindfulness, do not know they are different, albeit related concepts.

The relationship between mindfulness and meditation is similar to the relationship between fitness and exercise. When you go to the gym and exercise, you are not working out so that you will be more fit at the gym but instead so you have a higher level of fitness when you are outside the gym. It is the same with meditation. You do formal meditation practices not so that you are more mindful during the exercises but so you are more mindful in your everyday life. Meditation is a mental exercise that affects your baseline level of mindfulness just like physical exercise affects your baseline level of fitness. However, not all meditations are created equal.

The comparison of physical exercise to meditation is relevant for several reasons. When you think of the term "exercise," what comes to mind? You might think of jumping jacks, push-ups, jogging, squats, sit-ups, burpees, westernized yoga, pull-ups, bench presses, lunges, sprints, intervals, and the list could go on. You might also consider your overall fitness goals in determining which exercises you would choose to do. For example, if you were looking to build strength in your chest and back, you would likely want to incorporate bench presses and pull-ups into your overall workout plan. If, however, you were looking to improve your running speed and endurance, you might choose to incorporate sprints and intervals into your routine and perhaps even avoid some exercises because they may be counterproductive for achieving your fitness goals. It makes total sense to do that. It also makes sense to do that with meditation because not all meditations are mindfulness meditations.

Similar to the term "exercise," "meditation" represents a large family of practices that have different outcomes and are not necessarily complementary. For example, I could guide you in an elaborate meditation in which I describe a situation when you are walking along a pristine beach. You can hear the waves lapping on the shore rhythmically as the ocean spray catches the deep orange color of the setting sun and a slightly warm breeze brushes along your skin. That could be a powerful meditation that relaxes you, but it is a visualization meditation, not a mindfulness meditation. I could give you a syllable, word, or phrase to continuously repeat in your mind or out loud. That may be a potent meditation to get you into particular mental states or trances, but it is a mantra or chanting meditation, not a mindfulness meditation; Transcendental Meditation fits into this category. I could guide you in a meditation in which I have you imagine family members, friends, or anyone you have deep feelings of love and compassion for and then have you deliberately draw forth and intensify those feelings. That could be a helpful meditation to cultivate higher levels of compassion and kindness, but that is a lovingkindness meditation, not a mindfulness meditation. In other words, if you want strong legs, you do squats and lunges. And if you want to reap the benefits recent research suggests are associated with mindfulness, it behooves you to do meditations that genuinely affect your base level of mindfulness. To cultivate mindfulness, you do mindfulness meditations.

These non-mindfulness meditations just described have a number of benefits, to be sure, but most are routinely, inadvertently, or intentionally marketed as if they are mindfulness-enhancing meditations when they are not. I provide and promote some non-mindfulness meditations in my training, as you will see in Part II. The difference is that I will make the distinction between mindfulness and non-mindfulness meditations and be fully transparent with you about what exercises we are doing and why, versus lumping everything under the moniker "mindfulness" to hoodwink people into buying something. I wish more people who are ostensibly in the business of helping others would be more honest about which meditations and exercises are mindfulness meditations and which are not.

There are some sure-fire ways to know if a meditation is a mindfulness meditation or not. Notice whether the meditation is deliberately adding or pushing away something from your experience, and if it does, it is not a mindfulness meditation. Mindfulness meditations ask you to notice your experience as it is in the present moment versus changing it. If a meditation is asking you to breathe in a certain pattern such as 4/7/8 breathing or box breathing, it is not a mindfulness meditation. Heck, it is not even a meditation; it is a breathing exercise! Mindfulness meditations never ask you to change your breathing pattern or rate. If a meditation is trying to make you feel a certain way such as compassionate or relaxed, it is not a mindfulness meditation. Mindfulness meditations encourage you to notice whatever emotions or states of being are arising in the moment and acknowledge them, not try to change them or turn away from them. If a meditation is accompanied by phrases such as "clear your mind" or "stop all thoughts," you know two things; your teacher is not a mindfulness teacher (or is an inexperienced one) and you are not doing a mindfulness meditation. Mindfulness meditations are not trying to get you to stop all thoughts. Asking your brain to stop thinking is like asking your lungs to stop breathing and is just about as useful. We are not seeking to eliminate thinking on our journey to being more mindful. We are cultivating a new relationship with thoughts, one in which we are less affected or pushed around by unskillful and unhelpful thoughts.

What meditations do cultivate mindfulness? There are two primary types of meditations that, used in tandem, develop and deepen mindfulness: focused attention and open monitoring. We will describe and practice focused attention further on in the chapter but will only describe open monitoring, which we won't practice until Part II.

Focused Attention Meditation

The most basic meditation to begin the journey to cultivating mindfulness is focused attention meditation, which increases your ability to concentrate and keep your attention where you want it to be. This is the practice of intentionally directing your attention to a particular object, sometimes called an "anchor," and when you notice the mind has wandered, you return attention to the object. It's that simple, although it is not necessarily easy, as you will see shortly. Remember, in mindfulness meditations, we do not add or take anything away from our experience during the practice. Therefore, we will not be going out to find or buy an object to do this practice. We do not need to go find a spiritual teacher to give us a special phrase to focus on, we do not have to run to the store to get a candle and matches so we have a flame to stare into, and we do not need to get a bell or "singing" bowl to ring to focus on the sound. To do a focused attention meditation aimed at affecting mindfulness, we will choose an anchor we have with us at all times: the breath.

Most of us overlook the process of breathing nearly every moment of our lives, that is, until something comes along and hinders the process, then we begin to pay very close attention to the breath whether we want to or not. Fortunately, despite our lack of awareness of (and gratitude for) our breath, it has kept us company from the day we drew that first strained breath after leaving our mother's womb to this very moment. Consequently, from a convenience perspective, it is the ultimate "object" to use for a focused attention meditation; you never have to remember to bring it!

When you do a focused attention meditation and the object of the meditation is the breath, it is called an Awareness of Breath meditation. You can do this as a formal exercise; for example, you set aside a specific amount of time for the practice (5, 10, 20, 30, 45 minutes), sit in a chair, and do the exercise. You can also do this as an informal exercise, for example, when you are waiting for an elevator and you spontaneously decide to focus on your breath for a few moments. We will do this as a quick formal practice now and I recommend doing it at least 10 to 15 minutes a day.

You can read through the following meditation transcript and then do the exercise on your own without any guidance. However, especially if you are new to this, I recommend doing it as a guided meditation by listening to the audio files noted in the Resources, my teacher account on the Insight Timer app, or at http://www.clifsmith. com; see the Appendix for details. The audio guidance will help you stay on track until you are comfortable and/or interested in doing the exercise on your own.

Awareness of Breath Meditation

The most basic way to do a mindfulness meditation is simply to focus your attention on your breath, the inhale and exhale, and anytime your mind wanders away. Just notice what your mind got caught in, release it, and bring your attention back to noticing the sensations of breathing. Be gentle with yourself as you are probably new to this. The most important thing is to bring a sense of curiosity and patience to the experience. Let's begin.

♦ Find a comfortable place where you can sit for a few minutes. You do not have to sit in lotus position on a meditation cushion; sitting on a chair will work equally well. Sit up straight but relaxed and allow your feet to be flat on the floor. The rationale for sitting up straight is to remain awake and alert for the exercise. You can place your hands in your lap or wherever is most comfortable. You don't have to hold your hands in any special way.

♦ Allow your eyes to close if that feels comfortable for you; otherwise, lower your gaze down at about a 45-degree angle and soften your focus. The reason for closing your eyes for this particular practice is to eliminate visual distractions.

♦ Bring your attention now to noticing the sensations of the breath wherever you feel them most distinctly. You might feel the sensations of air moving in and out of your nose as you breathe in and breathe out. You might notice sensations associated with the rising and falling of your chest or abdomen each time you inhale and exhale. Sensations of breathing in any of those areas are perfectly fine to focus on for the exercise.

♦ If you have some difficulty noticing the sensations of breathing, go ahead and take one or two deeper breaths intentionally, just to get a sense of what these sensations feel like and where you might focus your attention. Then release any impulse to control or change your breathing. Remember this is not a breathing exercise; this is an exercise in attention and awareness.

◆ Now just noticing the sensations of breathing as the breath breathes itself. Paying close attention to the sensations for the full duration of each inbreath and full duration of each outbreath.

◆ You might find, after a short time, that your mind has wandered away from the breath to a thought or judgment, such as a judgment about the exercise or a thought about what you have to do later today. When this happens, it is not a mistake. You have not done anything wrong. Just notice what your mind got caught up in and gently but firmly escort your attention back to noticing the sensations of breathing.

◆ The mind will get caught up in thinking over and over again. Whether this happens 50, 500, or 5,000 times, just acknowledge where the mind went and guide your attention back to the breath every time. No need to harshly criticize yourself for getting lost in thought; this is the practice.

◆ Open your eyes if you've closed them and bring your attention back into the room you're in. Give yourself a moment to get your bearings before moving into the next part of your day.

I think it is logical to ask, "What the heck can following the breath for 10 to 15 minutes a day actually do?" Consistently practicing this exercise leads to an increased ability to intentionally sustain attention on any object or task. On the surface level, this is a practical skill as we navigate our distracted and overstimulated world. On a deeper level, the additional power of concentration and stability of mind also become a crucially important set of tools when we move to noticing the various nuances of our experience with a higher level of clarity, leading to a deeper understanding of and wiser responses to our lives. Furthermore, attending to the breath in this way begins to help us perceive, and become more comfortable with, the continuous changing nature of all things.

Because some of the benefits and outcomes noted in the previous paragraph are somewhat abstract, here are some specific results from survey data captured in the 8-week mindful leadership courses I've led over the last 5 years. Although I cannot disclose all the data and survey questions, I can provide insights into a handful of the key impacts we have measured. These data were collected using participant self-report surveys taken prior to course kickoff and 2 weeks after the completed course; results reflect changes in the average scores for the entire group of participants. Please note, these changes occurred across the entire course, which includes focused attention, open monitoring, as well as other exercises and meditations.

- 39% increased energy level
- 24% increased ability to think more clearly
- 33% increase in sense of compassion
- 13% increase in ability to take a more balanced view of things
- 14% increase in job satisfaction
- 21% reduction in rumination

The results speak for themselves but let's drill into a couple to drive home a few points about impact. Take the 21% reduction in rumination as our first example. If you have ever wondered why the best elite athletes have regular mindfulness practices, reduction in rumination and other unhelpful internal dialogue is one of the key reasons. Can you imagine, a Major League Baseball pitcher steps on the pitcher's mound. He eyes his opponent and launches his best pitch, a fastball. The batter swings powerfully and the fans hear the familiar crack of a well-hit ball. The pitcher knows immediately it is a home run. Can you imagine what would happen to the confidence and performance of the pitcher during the next set of pitches and batters if that pitcher was caught up in rumination about the "stupid mistake" he made? Would that athlete even be in the Major League? Not a chance with that level of an untrained mind.

The 14% increase in job satisfaction is also one worth examining a bit. I do not know if a 14% increase over 2 months is impressive, because I am not aware of any other courses that attempt to measure impact on job satisfaction over such a short period of time. Most employer job satisfaction surveys are conducted annually after a year's worth of culture or other training and actions have been taken to improve it. What I do believe is worth mentioning about the jump in job satisfaction is that I did not call up the leaders senior to the course participants and ask, "Hey, could you take it easy on the individuals taking this training over the next 8 weeks; getting good outcomes in pre- and post-course surveys is important. Be a bit nicer to them and please don't make them work nights and weekends or have them work on client proposals over long holiday breaks." These

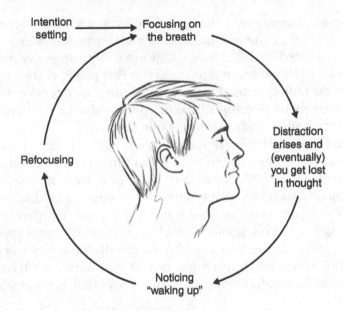

FIGURE 6.1 AWARENESS OF BREATH MEDITATION CYCLE.
Source: From 99designs.com/Konstantin. Reprinted with permissions of 99designs.com.

participants had the same jobs, workload, and bosses they had prior to the class, but by merely learning a bit more about how their brain works and by training it in a new way, they had a better experience at work. In addition, anecdotally based on participant emails, many participants say their home life also improved significantly.

How could something as simple as noticing the sensations of breathing contribute to results such as these? Let's break down the exercise into its constituent parts and look at what skills you are building in each phase of an Awareness of Breath meditation. Take a look at Figure 6.1 for an overview of the cycle of the exercise.

INTENTION SETTING

First, just before we begin the exercise, we set our intention for it. We've decided to do an Awareness of Breath meditation and so keeping our attention on the breath is our intention. We do this prior to the exercise to prime ourselves and be deliberate about how we will spend the next moments of our day. Setting an intention and being deliberate about our time is not something most of us do regularly. We may have a vague idea of what we want to accomplish at work or at home but as we start our day we are quickly waylaid by the "tyranny of the urgent." Those fire drills, emails from the boss, the colleague coming by your desk to tell you about the latest policy change, and other things that pull us away from our vague idea of what we wanted to do. There's a double whammy; we were not clear about what we wanted to do in the first place, and so it's much easier to be pulled away. Deliberately setting an intention for these exercises helps us develop this skill and enables us to more readily set intentions across other areas of our lives.

I must issue a clarification and caveat here. There are two types of intention often associated with mindfulness practice. One intention with a capital "I" (Intention) and one with a lowercase "i" (intention). Lowercase "i" intention is for your individual practice, for example, pay attention to the breath. Capital "I" Intention is for your overall reason or goal for picking up a mindfulness practice in the first place. Maybe you have heard mindfulness can lower your stress and that is what you want out of it. Maybe you have heard mindfulness can help calm a busy mind and that is what you want out of it.

Now that the clarification is made, on to the caveat. Capital "I" Intentions are very useful to keep your practice consistent, particularly when you do not feel like practicing. Reminding yourself of your Intention can help you get out of bed in the morning and do your practice even if you do not feel like it. It can help you pick your practice back up after a few missed days. That said, I recommend you hold your capital "I" Intentions lightly. One of the paradoxes of mindfulness practice is that when you hold too tightly to the intention or goal of your practice it can actually drive you further from "achieving" it. Say, for example your overall Intention for starting a diligent mindfulness practice is to have more presence of mind and not be lost in thought so much when you are spending time with your family. Holding tightly to that "I" Intention even during an individual practice can cause you some challenges. If your mind happens to be rather agitated during a particular individual meditation exercise (which is quite common even for experienced meditators), holding tightly to your Intention might cause you to say to yourself, "I'm supposed to be focused on the breath, and my mind is all over the place. I just need to be focused. I'm not good at this because my mind is racing." What is happening there? You are interjecting noise into the process due to wanting the exercise to go a certain way, to be exactly in line with your Intention and expectations, and because you are so fixated on the goal, you generate the additional inner noise pushing you further away from your Intention. So, bottom line, know your Intention, use it to keep your practice consistent, and hold it lightly most of the time.

FOCUS

Second, we focus our attention on the sensations of breathing. This ability to pay close attention to various aspects of our experience, such as perceiving cool air coming in the nose and warm air coming out, is an innate human skill we all have at varying degrees. As I mentioned, no one has cornered the market on mindfulness. Your ability to perceive your experience at more granular levels is yours, and it is your decision whether or not you are going to cultivate this skill. When you focus (and refocus) your attention on the breath, you are strengthening your ability to focus and concentrate. The ability to keep your attention where you want it to be is a key differentiator in a world full of distractions and deliberate attempts to hijack it.

NOTICING

Third, at some point after beginning to focus on your breath, you will realize you have been caught up in a stream of thoughts and thinking. There are two types of noticing here that can cause some confusion. You are noticing *that* you were lost in thought and noticing *what* you were lost in. The first noticing is passive; it happens to you. You suddenly notice you were lost in thought. The second noticing is more active; it is noticing what your mind got caught up in. I will use the term "acknowledging" to mean this second type of noticing to avoid the confusion. So, you notice you were lost in thought and acknowledge what you got caught up in.

You may get lost in a thought stream about your to-do list and what is next on it. It could be judgments and commentary about the exercise itself. It may turn out to be a more elaborate story than you would expect to happen during a meditation. You might think of your daughter, which leads you to think about her boyfriend. You note you do not like that kid very much and consider what you would do to him if he mistreats her. Then you think, "Well, if I did that, I'd probably have a run-in with the police." Ten minutes further into this story and you are planning how you would escape from prison, in your own personal version of *Shawshank Redemption*. This is what the mind does. It proliferates thought after thought after thought. It is similar to when we go online "just to check email" and 20 minutes later we are doing deep research into Illuminati conspiracy theories. What pulls you in could be a million other things that tend to pop into our minds at any given time, especially when we pause all outward activity to practice something like mindfulness meditation. The first point to take away here is that this is completely normal and inevitable! You will get lost in thought. As you begin to do these exercises more regularly, it will become abundantly clear how quickly and easily we are taken in by the random vagaries of arising thoughts. When you "wake up" and notice you were lost in thought, *that* is a moment of mindfulness. As soon as you notice it, you are already back. That is like "waking up" while driving and realizing you missed a few miles. It does not mean, necessarily, that the thought stream is gone; the thought stream may remain for a time. However, now you are standing back from the thought, where it can be acknowledged, instead of being "lost" within it.

Acknowledging the thought is simply taking note of the content of the thought stream that caught you, not writing it down or saying to yourself, "I was thinking about my daughter's boyfriend." Just take note of it. What happens, over time, is that you become more aware of your own habits of mind and patterns of thinking. You see, much of your behavior is driven by thoughts and beliefs that are hovering below the surface of your conscious awareness. If you practice consistently, some of these habits and patterns will rise to the level of your conscious awareness. Once you are aware of something, you can do something about it.

Refocusing

Fourth, after noticing and acknowledging the thoughts or stories you got caught up in, gently but firmly guide your attention back to focusing on the sensations of breathing. There is no need to criticize yourself for getting caught up in a thought stream. This is absolutely normal. If you beat yourself up every time you get lost in thought, you will get better at self-criticism, which is something most of us already do too well. Harsh self-criticism and self-attack are often common habits of the mind and, in Part II, we will discuss ways to reduce these unhelpful habits while preserving the ability for thoughtful reflection on how we can show up as our best selves in any context.

When you refocus your attention on the sensations of breathing you are simultaneously practicing the skill of letting go of a thought stream. This is one of the most important skills a diligent and consistent mindfulness practice cultivates. I imagine you have been in an argument, or many, at some point in your life. Some of those arguments probably lasted only 2 or 3 minutes but then for the next 2 or 3 hours or *days* you are still ruminating on the argument and coming up with comebacks you really wish you would have used in it. If not used in that argument, perhaps you decide to put those comebacks in your back pocket for the next argument you already anticipate having in the future. Wouldn't it be great to be able to set those ruminating thoughts down and focus on what is right in front of you? In another scenario we often find ourselves in, perhaps you are just trying to get a good night's sleep but you had a dust-up with someone at work and you cannot stop thinking about it, which is keeping you wide awake. Wouldn't it be better to be able to set those thoughts down, get a good night's sleep, and pick them up the next day when you could actually do something about the situation? That is a skill you will be cultivating every time you do this exercise and bring your attention back to the sensations of breathing. Please note, we are not eliminating thoughtful reflection here but instead reducing the impact of unhelpful rumination.

To recap the four basic steps of focused attention meditation:

Intention Setting for the meditation (held lightly and set just before starting the practice)
Focusing on the object/anchor (sensations of breathing)
Noticing *that* you were lost in thought and *what* you got caught in
Refocusing your attention back on the object/anchor

Open Awareness Meditation

In contrast to focused attention meditation, open awareness, also known as "open monitoring" meditation, does not attempt to privilege or intentionally focus on any one particular object or aspect of our experience. Instead, the practice is to notice and be open to whatever arises in our general field of awareness, notice what enters the spotlight of attention and takes the main stage of awareness, and notice when it leaves the main stage and what it is replaced by. This meditation is sometimes more challenging so I will be incorporating this practice in Part II, after you have had time to build up practice with different types of focused attention meditations.

■ ■ ■

We covered a great deal of ground in this chapter. We learned that, just like there are many beneficial forms of exercise, there are many types of meditation, and just as we must choose certain exercises that will affect our physical fitness in specific ways, we must choose to practice mindfulness meditations that will increase our baseline level of mindfulness. We discussed that non-mindfulness meditations are not inherently bad; in fact, some have very well documented benefits, but they may not be doing what recent research suggests mindfulness meditations do, and therefore mislabeling them as mindfulness is unhelpful for anyone looking to reap the scientifically validated benefits of mindfulness. We covered the two key mindfulness meditations—focused attention and open monitoring—as well as some of the skills you cultivate when practicing a focused attention meditation such as Awareness of Breath.

Now that we have a basic understanding of the fundamentals of mindfulness, let's close out Part I with the next chapter and prepare to move into the 8-week course where the real learning and impact begin.

Chapter 7

Your Journey

We kicked off Part I of this book with a description of how paying closer attention to what I was doing with my own mind and committing to training it has enabled me to move from poverty to prosperity. Being dealt the random hand of being born into a poor family, living in a trailer with no college-educated family members, and being raised by a single mother of three could have resulted in a much different journey and life. I must be honest here that mindfulness was not the only thing that affected my journey; there was also preparation, hard work, continuous learning, surrounding myself with people who challenged me to grow, and, of course, good luck and timing. That said, mindfulness, Catch and Release, and other self-developed techniques I'll share in Part II played outsized roles in influencing my ability to see more clearly and respond to life thoughtfully as opposed to buying into the story the mind automatically makes up in reaction to the countless number of life situations we regularly face that require us to make choices. Those individual responses and choices seemed small, even insignificant, at the time. However, just like small financial investments grow large with interest compounding over time, clear seeing, thoughtful responses, and wise choices compound, leading to a massive impact on your trajectory and experience of life.

So, let's talk a bit about your journey for a moment. You are also on an unknown but promising journey through this life, and it will be filled with achievements, accolades, and love. You will get that promotion, win that business deal, marry the one you love, and reach many of your goals. And, yet, you will also have your share of stumbles, failures, and heartbreak. Undoubtedly, you have already faced some challenges in your life, things you wish would have gone differently, a mistake you wish you could change, a love lost, or a hurtful comment hurled that you would take back if you could. One of the most pernicious beliefs is that life is meant to be perfect. Setbacks and unmet expectations are common human experiences as we find our way through this life; they are not signs that our life is bad. Therefore, I encourage you to be fully present for all those difficult experiences because, just as you cannot truly know the experience of something sweet without the experience of tasting something sour, it's our challenges and failures in life that make our achievements so fulfilling.

Also, don't miss all the small subtle and seemingly trivial moments between your "honey-do" lists, daily work tasks, and lofty professional goals. Those goals and tasks are important, to be sure, just like the finale is a very important part of a symphony, but the goal is not to get to the end of the symphony as fast as possible. Each note, high or low, and even the silence between the notes, are the whole point. Without each of those elements, we would not have any music at all (or it would be exceedingly dull). Can you imagine a symphony or a song with only high notes and no spaces of silence? This concept is also expressed in other things, such as climbing or dancing. The point of climbing Mount Everest is not merely to get to the top and see the views. People who share their stories of climbing Everest don't just describe the last 10 feet; they share the challenges, the setbacks, the lucky breaks, the fear, the self-doubt, and the triumph. The point of dancing isn't to get to a certain point on the dance floor as if you are following a map to the beach. The point is in the dancing itself.[1] So, enjoy your journey. It's going to look something like what is shown in Figure 7.1.

It's not going to look like your plan or your expectation and that's okay. Each of those moments, high or low, is a note in the symphony of your life. Be present for them. Be grateful for them. You don't want to get to the end of your journey, like the end of that car ride, having missed most of it because you were lost in thought.

Mindfulness is not merely going to improve your emotional intelligence and make you a better leader. It's not just going to help you navigate the ups and downs of life with a bit more poise, grace, and ease even when under high-pressure situations. It's not just going to help you get a handle on your stress and automatic reactivity. It's not just going to help you Catch and Release unhelpful internal

Your plan

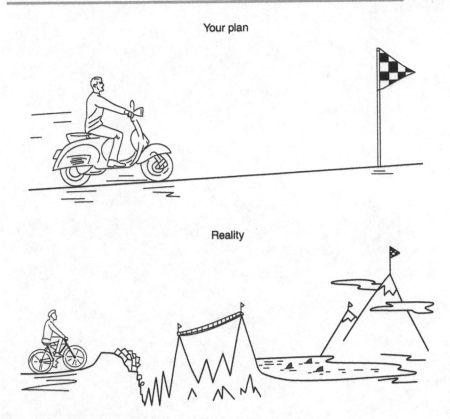

Reality

FIGURE 7.1 PLAN VERSUS REALITY.

Source: From 99designs.com/Konstantin. Reprinted with permissions of 99designs.com.

thoughts and beliefs that keep you from realizing your full potential. It will do all those things, but what it will also do is help you greet the last moments of your journey knowing that you were awake for the whole show. And that, dear reader, is one of the sweetest fruits of mindfulness.

In order to grow and reap that fruit, we must sow the seed of mindfulness. If you've read this far, you have that seed in your hand right now. What are you going to do with it? Be content to just understand it superficially or take the disciplined steps to cultivate it? In Part II, we'll plant, water, and provide sunlight to that seed so it can grow into a powerful ally on your journey to exceptional performance, leadership, and well-being. Are you ready to begin?

Part II

Diving Deeper: An 8-Week Journey to Exceptional Performance, Leadership, and Well-Being

Chapter 8

Introducing the Course

First, let me congratulate you for taking this initial step on the journey of planting and nurturing the seed of mindfulness that's now in your hand. It is a courageous act to turn the spotlight of attention inwardly because during this process it is highly likely we will come across some things that might be difficult to accept, but accept them we must, lest we wish to remain shackled by our past.

Part II of this book is designed to guide you through the process of developing a consistent, diligent, and sustained mindfulness meditation practice through which you can reap the scientifically validated benefits of mindfulness. Throughout the remaining chapters, I will introduce various practices, exercises, and activities intended to bring about a transformational shift in how you navigate, interact with, and experience your world in a way that leads to unlocking and enhancing your own latent talents. The core themes of each chapter will not only encompass mindfulness but also, where appropriate, weave in useful philosophical, performance enhancement, and leadership principles. Don't worry, I will clearly call this out so as to avoid diluting or misrepresenting core tenets of mindfulness.

The next chapters will follow a structured flow designed to enable you to pick up the concepts quickly, practice effectively, and apply learnings in real-life situations. I'll first discuss the key concept(s) of the chapter and why they are important. Then we will transition to the main practice, a 10- to 20-minute meditation, which will be part of your daily "homework" (along with various other insight- or skill-building activities we'll introduce). Starting in week 2, I'll include a section called "Common Themes, Challenges, and Questions" to address situations that tend to come up not long after one starts to practice. Finally, each chapter will end with a "Key Points, Practices, and Signposts" section which will include major highlights, your daily practices, and some signposts to help you notice where you might see mindfulness making an impact on your life.

Because I've mentioned noticing impact of your practice, I must note that this is not a quick fix. Hoping to see massive change after a day or two of mindfulness practice is like exercising in the gym for the first time and then immediately rushing home to look at yourself in the mirror to see how much healthier you look. This isn't a Google search; results don't come immediately. I highly recommend you commit to completing this course and focus primarily on doing the practices consistently and pay less attention on the outcomes. In my experience, it's often people around you who will notice the positive changes first and then ask about them.

Each chapter represents a week of practice. You can spend more time doing the main practice in each chapter, that is, spending 2 weeks doing the main practice of each chapter before moving on to the next, but I would recommend against spending less time. These exercises build on one another in a way that leads to compounding insights and growth in much the same way as interest in a retirement account compounds little by little and then suddenly the numbers really begin to grow. Jumping straight to the exercises in the last chapter of the course, or skipping "investment" in some chapters, is detrimental to your learning along this particular path.

Of course, you can read the entire book so you have a broader understanding before beginning the course, but you must go back to start the course and do the exercises to reap the benefits. Reading the entire book will give you an intellectual understanding of some of the key concepts and insights but an intellectual understanding is not enough. In a similar way, you could read a book about the best swimming strokes for speed or stamina but until you jump in the water and start swimming, your skill level has not been affected one iota.

■ ■ ■

As with incorporating any new activity into our lives we will need to commit to and make room for the practices in this course. When we try to change our routine, our minds will intervene to try to stop us. It's best to acknowledge this now and take steps to minimize the impact. Remember that New Year's resolution you made but it didn't stick? You know the one. You got up early in the morning every day for about a week to do your thing and then, in week 2, your alarm went off but you did not get up. What happened?

This is an all-too-common experience for most of us. When we try to incorporate a new behavior into our lives, we rarely intentionally decide what might need to be sacrificed to make the time nor do we effectively commit to and attach the new behavior to something we are already doing. As a result, on that fateful morning noted above, your mind made up an excuse as to why you should skip getting up early that day—and you bought it hook, line, and sinker and hit the snooze button. After that happened, your "resolution" didn't stand a chance of becoming a consistent behavior.

Your mind will attempt to do this to you during this course, so let's uncover your motivation; decide what needs to give; pick a time, place, and cue for our main practice; understand what to do when the mind tries to beguile us with its various excuses to keep us small and in our comfortable routines; and form a strong commitment now.

Motivation

Why are you reading this book? Why are you taking this course? What do you hope you get from this practice and why? Take 5 minutes and write down the answer to these questions. It is extremely valuable to understand your motivation, at least at a basic level, for committing to a consistent mindfulness practice. Are you looking to be able to be steadier under pressure? Do you want to be more present with your loved ones in a world full of distraction? Is an enhanced ability to fully face and navigate the inevitable ups and downs of life why you are embarking on this journey? Whatever the answers to these questions, it's important to be as specific as possible. The more precise your understanding, the more helpful it will be when your willpower wanes. Although we want to hold these motivations and goals lightly, you can allow the answers to these questions to be touchstones you come back to on the days you don't feel like practicing.

What Do You Need to Give Up?

Time for this course will not magically appear, so what must you adjust to create the time and who needs to know about it? One place to create this time is to look at what you are already practicing that might be an unwise (or less helpful) use of your limited time. Whether you are aware of it or not, you are already practicing many things in your life that might not be serving you well. Perhaps you're regularly practicing procrastination by "doom-scrolling" on social media for 2 hours a day. Maybe you're practicing being a gossip by spending time at work talking about other people instead of completing work-related tasks. Are you practicing being the best at pop culture trivia by watching every season of the latest and greatest shows on your favorite streaming or cable service? These "practices" not only take up your precious time but also they are reinforcing those neuropathways we discussed previously, making it easier and easier to fall into those unhelpful habits. Everything you do has an opportunity cost. Why not replace some of those "practices" with some practices that can make a positive difference in your personal and professional life? Spend a few minutes conducting an inventory of when you have 20 to 30 minutes of time that could be taken from something unhelpful and be reallocated to the mindfulness practices and exercises in this course. When you have come up with a few things you could adjust (and there are always a few) ask yourself if anyone in your life needs to know about you doing this course and how can that person support you. Letting your spouse, partner, roommates, children, coworkers, or friends know that you want to commit to this course and sharing how they can support you can mean the difference between making the time to do the practices or making excuses.

Establishing the Practice

Let's get real. The best time to think about where and what you are going to do to exercise is not at 5:30 am when your alarm is buzzing. That's a recipe for disaster. BJ Fogg and James Clear are well-known authors for their books on how to develop habits that stick, so we will leverage some of their techniques for our practice.[1] I highly recommend both their books but personally do not like the term "habit" because it implies doing something mindlessly and without thinking, which is essentially the opposite of mindfulness, so will use the term "behavior" in the place of "habit" here. Fogg and Clear offer some common themes that help people successfully establish new behaviors. It is critical to create an environment conducive to the new behavior, including easy-to-notice cues to trigger it. They advocate for clearly describing and writing down when and where the behavior is to take place. Linking the new behavior to existing behaviors can be helpful as well, and both authors are adamant about celebrating or rewarding oneself for doing the new behavior. Let's bring some of these themes into our context.

What would a clear and detailed written statement look like for a new behavior? A sample commitment statement in the context of our purposes could be something like, "Every morning, after I start brewing my coffee, I will do my main mindfulness practice for 10 minutes at the kitchen table." This statement has the cue/current behavior, new behavior, where it will be done, and for how long. Seems pretty specific to me. Another one could be, "Each night, when I place my toothbrush in its holder after brushing, I will walk to the living room and do 15 minutes of mindfulness meditation."

What cues can serve as triggers for new behaviors? It could be anything, but it needs to be easy to see and understand. If your new behavior is running, you might lay out your exercise clothes and running shoes beside your bed so you see them first. For mindfulness, you might simply have a yellow sticky note on your mirror or on the coffee pot where you will see it every day. Maybe you change your phone background to say "Did you do your daily mindfulness practice?" so you have a cue readily available in the case you missed the practice the first time around or to serve as a reminder to do informal practice throughout the day. This is when some people decide to bring in images, accessories, or other items stereotypically associated with mindfulness, such as tiny statues of the Buddha, prayer/meditation beads, bells, and so on to serve as reminders to practice.

Don't forget the reward. Each day you do the practice celebrate or reward yourself in some small way. How do you celebrate small wins currently? Do you text a friend or accountability buddy? Do you do a fist pump in the air? Do you treat yourself to your favorite coffee? Incorporate a reward or celebration that evokes positive feelings to further reinforce the new behavior. This is not to say the actual meditation has to be pleasurable; in fact, it may be very difficult, like working out hard in the gym might be very uncomfortable. In both instances, it's still worth celebrating the fact you did the exercises.

Okay, take 5 minutes to come up with and write down a preliminary practice statement outlining the when, where, and how long you will practice, what cue(s) you can incorporate, and how you will celebrate or reward yourself for doing the daily exercise.

Dealing with the Excuse-Making, Judging, and Controlling Mind

When you begin this course, your mind is not going to like it. You've been conditioned your entire life to be seeking something outside yourself to satisfy something inside yourself. When you were 4 years old you wanted a piece of candy, at 6 you wanted a bike, at 16 it was a car, at 18 it was the right university, at 22 you wanted to land that amazing job, at 30 the house and family, at 35 the promotion, and it continues to this day. Happiness, self-worth, and fulfillment always seem to be on the other side of the next achievement or acquisition and the mind is in the driver's seat. Ask anyone who has ever had to take the car keys away from an elderly parent or grandparent because of unsafe driving how the older person reacts. They do not like it and, sometimes, they threaten, argue, and retaliate. You can expect some of the same behavior from your mind.

Your mind is not going to like you taking even 10 minutes out of your day to "do nothing" but "waste time." Oh, you may start out strong and motivated but, at some point, the mind will begin to chime in with its judgments about how things are going, creating excuses for skipping practice, and then issuing sweet whispers about how you've advanced way beyond this course or these practices and so you can stop. It will, at times, complain that you are not good at this and that you have better things to do. You'll have a meditation session in which your mind is all over the place, thoughts going this way and that, and then the mind will begin to bombard you with thoughts of being a failure. The mind will be doing all of these things for one reason and one reason alone: to remain in charge.

It is unclear to me who originally said, "The mind is an excellent servant but a terrible master," but the sentiment here captures the situation. Over the next 2 months you will be learning about and exercising your mind in a new way and, if done consistently and diligently, it will flip this power dynamic. Your mind knows this and will throw everything at you to make you stop. Do not give in. Use the Catch and Release technique I taught you in Part I so you can do what you committed to and not fall prey to the tyranny of the excuse-making, judging, and controlling mind. Catch those thoughts and meet them with the curiosity of a scientist and the same kindness and compassion you would extend to a true friend and then Release them. In time, you will begin to see the thoughts that bubble up into your head just come and go like clouds in the sky. They are not what you are, and you don't need to give them power over your actions or take them personally. This may sound a little strange at this point but you will begin to truly know what I mean as your practice time increases. As you begin to free yourself from the tyranny of the mind, your self-limiting beliefs hold less power over you, your automatic reactivity to life begins to diminish, and you will find a new space from which to engage with the world. Eventually, you will begin to realize a simpler, yet deeper, definition of mindfulness: the felt understanding that mindfulness is a conversation with the present moment when only the moment is doing the talking.

Chapter 9

Week 1: No Trivial Moments

MOVING FROM AUTOPILOT TO AWARE

Two years ago, when I heard of the tragic death of a young boy in our neighborhood, I had just finished presenting a several-week-long series of mindfulness classes and was relaxing and trying to be present with my own son at our campsite just outside Gettysburg, Pennsylvania. The news shook me like any news of child-related tragedies often shake parents. I was genuinely despondent and yet simultaneously grateful my son was safe. I'm sure the out-of-the-blue hug I gave him lasted a little too long and was a little too tight for his 3-year-old body to contend with so he wriggled out and went back to digging up our plants to find whatever bugs lived beneath them.

My mind immediately ran an imaginary reel of how the events of that day may have unfolded for the working parents, conjuring up the associated emotions in the process:

Mom or dad drops off the child at school on the way to work, doing it in a rush to get to the office more quickly. Stuck in traffic, annoyed it took too long for drop-off again, committing to a plan to streamline the process. Going through the workday dealing with tasks, getting frustrated at ineffective processes, and venting with colleagues about the boss's latest "good idea." Sitting in the sterile office of the future-style cube, scanning emails on the all-too-slow work laptop that they've been battling with IT for weeks to replace. Wanting to save time at lunch, they continue scanning email and barely taste their meal before rushing on to the next meeting. Then, a curious feeling arises at noticing the school calling and thinking, "Did I forget to pack his lunch? Did he forget to tell me they only have half-day at school, and now I'm going to have to drop everything and pick him up?" As the caller speaks, all the aforementioned frustrations and concerns about being inconvenienced vanish in a tidal wave of pain, disbelief, anger, and deep sadness.

I cry. The imaginary reel jumps forward.

The disappearance of work-related problems makes way for an unquenchable longing to have back even one brief trivial moment with the child, whether it was annoying, frustrating, or uncontrollable. A parallel desire arises to access memories of trivial moments to which, it now becomes painfully clear, little if any conscious attention was paid at the time.

I look over at my son squishing dirt through his fingers I know I will need to help clean off before we eat dinner, intentionally taking in as much of the scene as I can.

It's an open secret that experiencing the tragedy of loss tends to rip back the heavy curtains of what society holds up as most important, namely, acquiring expensive things and achieving fame, and it reveals what is truly meaningful. In a flash, it becomes clear that genuine connection with the most important people in our lives is what touches us most deeply and it's precisely what we often take for granted. What's less apparent is that for most of us, this clearer view lasts only for a short time before we slowly and unconsciously, or perhaps are pressured to, ease back into our habitual behaviors.

We begin again to sacrifice genuine presence with others to multitask or focus on achieving society's version of success. This drifting back to a lack of authentic presence with others robs us of the many gifts that accompany true interpersonal connection. When the next inevitable catastrophe occurs, we are struck again with the clear view of what is truly important to us. However, this time, the view comes with a dose of self-criticism for again missing so many precious moments while knowing full well what truly matters.

Fortunately, we can learn from the tragedies, catastrophes, and losses, big and small, in our lives. We can use them as reminders to stay present with what's most important. When you realize the last time you dressed your child was *the* last time because the child can now do it alone and you wish you had paid more attention to those moments, that's a reminder. When you realize the last time you bathed your child was *the* last time and wish you could do it once more but your child won't let you, that's a reminder. Noticing these regularly occurring reminders will help you pay closer attention to the "trivial" moments in between. You know, the moments that make up most of your life. You also might begin to realize that moments are made trivial by not paying attention to them; when you pay close enough attention, moments cease to be trivial.

Back at the campground my reel continued, and I imagined what it must be like when you realize there are no longer any crumbs to clean up under your child's chair and you drop to your knees proclaiming with all your being that you would clean up crumbs for an eternity for just one more moment with your sweet angel.

I go sit with my son on the ground, dig my hands deep into the soil, and join in the most important moment of my life: the present moment.

$$\bullet \quad \bullet \quad \bullet$$

This story illustrates the changing value of "trivial moments" and the importance of being able to come off autopilot and purposefully bring attention to all moments of your life. Let's explore our tendency to move through life automatically and the implications of such behavior on our experiences, relationships, and decision-making.

We humans are creatures of habit and once something becomes routinized, it often fades into the background of experience. As we move through our lives, we slowly begin to run on automatic pilot. You've experienced this when you first started driving and, again, if you have ever moved to a new job and your commute changed. That first day driving required more focused attention and so you were very attentive to the entire experience. You noticed road signs, landmarks, and other cars. You paid close attention to where you placed your hands on the steering wheel and where your feet were aligned to press the gas or brake as appropriate. After a few months of driving, which is usually to the same set of locations, via the same routes, and at about the same times of day, you began to be able to pay attention to other things during the drive. You were able to think about a disagreement you had with a friend, listen to an audiobook, or plan your day, while the act of driving began to happen without paying much attention to the task.

This process is common and aligns with the four stages of competence described in psychology and paraphrased here.

- **Unconscious incompetence.** You don't know what you don't know.
- **Conscious incompetence.** You know you don't know.
- **Conscious competence.** You know and can do something if you focus on it.
- **Unconscious competence.** You can do it without even thinking about it.

The fact that we move through these stages when learning is an important aspect of being human and has evolutionary advantage. As we become unconsciously competent (on autopilot) when doing things, it frees up the brain to work on more difficult challenges or to come up with more innovative ideas. Additionally, we learned in the Part II introduction that the tying of one behavior to another that we already automatically do every day can make it easier to trigger and start the new behavior. This is true of automatic pilot as well. Sometimes our automatic behaviors can trigger the next series of behaviors that also become automatic. An example would be each time you grab your keys before leaving your house, you automatically check your pockets for your phone and wallet, then lock the front door, get in the car, turn on the car, and so on all without thinking. In these contexts and situations, it can seem like this process is universally good.

Unfortunately, autopilot also applies to behaviors that are not so beneficial and the distractions of the modern world exacerbate the problem. Have you ever been watching a movie and not realize you've eaten an entire bag of chips until you suddenly notice your hand grasping at empty space at the bottom of the bag? That's eating on autopilot, and you don't even get the "benefit" or joy of eating the snack! Have you noticed the habit of reaching for your phone? Most people have dozens of cues in their lives that trigger them to reach for their phones over 100 times a day without thinking about it.

Have to wait at a red light for 3 seconds? Check phone. Waiting in line at the store? Check phone. Just got into the car? Check phone. Parked the car? Check phone. Go to the bathroom? Check phone. That last one is kind of gross.

It goes beyond mere habits. We begin living much of our lives on autopilot and often fail to be aware of and attentive to our present moment experiences and the people around us. Autopilot can turn nearly all our moments into trivial moments. This automaticity creeps into our decision-making, our conversations, our leisure time, and even into our relationships. We all know what it's like to be with our loved ones, friends, or colleagues and not really be present with them because we are lost in thought or on our phones and just going through the motions of the interaction on autopilot.

In the chapter-opening story about the tragic loss of a child, we can imagine what the pain of being on autopilot with our loved ones might be like when we lose them. How much of your life is being lived on autopilot? How many moments of connection with others have you missed by having your attention automatically hijacked by your phone or by being lost in thought? How many of your moments have been turned into trivial moments by not paying attention to them?

■ ■ ■

Waking Up to Your Life

Mindfulness begins when we start to recognize the tendency to be on autopilot and take deliberate steps to wake up from it. To do that, we must begin to use our mindfulness "muscles," gain more agency over the direction of our attention, and strengthen those neural pathways in our brain so we can more easily come back to being mindful, focused, and responsive and operate from that mode of mind more often. We already started this process by doing the basic Awareness of Breath meditation I introduced in Chapter 6 on pages 56–59.

During the Awareness of Breath meditation, we followed the cycle of focusing attention on the sensations of breathing, noticing when we were lost in thought, and gently escorting attention back to the sensations of breathing. This is a core exercise and I recommend you do it at least twice a day throughout the course (and beyond) because of its effectiveness at focusing the mind and enhancing our ability to direct our attention at will. We call this type of exercise a formal practice. A formal practice is one in which we set aside specific time to do the meditation practice. It's like going to the gym to lift weights.

We will also do informal practices, which we do at other moments in the day and supports our overall mindfulness practice. Continuing with the fitness analogy, these exercises are like taking the stairs at work instead of the elevator because it supports your fitness goals. Informal practices do not replace formal practices; they complement them.

One important informal practice is to be more engaged in activities you currently do on automatic pilot. Common activities many of us do on autopilot are showering, brushing our teeth, snacking, making coffee, and many others you can probably come up with on your own. This type of informal practice is simply paying more attention and invoking all of your senses when doing one of these activities. Let's take showering as an example.

If I were to ask you how many people you shower with in the morning, you'd probably be stunned and maybe confused by the question. Eventually, you'd probably respond that you shower alone. However, I think that's not entirely true. It's likely that if you have meetings the day of your shower or an interview with someone, you'd probably be pre-living those interactions. If you've recently had a fight with your partner, you might be rehashing that conversation. In those moments you're not really alone in the shower, are you? You've brought in other people and situations and are not fully experiencing the shower. An informal practice here would be to deliberately notice the experience of showering through all your senses. This is taking a "mindful" shower.

Take a Mindful Shower

This evening or tomorrow morning when you take a shower, deliberately invoke all of your senses to experience the shower as fully as possible. The following instructions will give you an idea of how to carry out this informal practice. It helps to take a longer shower for this exercise and spend 5 to 10 seconds more on steps that you would usually do nearly instantly, but

continued

it's not something you have to do every time you want to take a mindful shower. Start just outside the shower before you even turn on the water.

1. **Seeing the shower.** Take moment to really look at the shower (tub/shower combo). Notice its shape, contour, and color. Look at the handle that controls the water flow and temperature. Allow yourself to explore each part before moving to the next step.

2. **Turning on the water.** Reach out to the handle and pay close attention to the exact moment your hand touches it. Notice what you feel? Is it cool to the touch? Smooth? Soft? Turn on the water.

3. **Hearing the water.** Listen to the full range of sounds that occur as you turn the shower on and adjust it to your desired temperature. Once the temperature is ready, step into the shower.

4. **Entering the shower.** Notice the feel of the water as it first touches your skin. Fully engage with the sense of touch. It may be very clear what the water feels like on your shoulders so close to the shower head. What does it feel like at your feet? Can you perceive the sensation of water at your feet? It's okay if you can't.

5. **Smelling the soap.** Grab your soap and hold it beneath your nose and inhale. What's the scent? Notice what impact it has on you. Is it pleasant? Is it powerful or subtle?

6. **Washing.** Lather up the soap and use it how you typically do to get clean. Notice the feel of the soap suds on your skin as well as any difference between the feeling of the soap in your hand and when it's lathered. Notice how you move from one body part to another, including your hair. Do you deliberately decide or does it happen automatically?

7. **Rinsing.** Deliberately place the soap/wash cloth back in its place. Notice how it feels to rinse the soap off your body. Fully engage with the sensations of the water washing down your body.

8. **Drying off.** Notice contrast when your wet hand touches the dry towel and be fully aware of the sensations where the towel meets the body as you dry yourself off.

9. **Noticing and reflecting.** When finished with the shower and after drying off, take a moment to notice any differences between the experience of taking a shower in this way and the way you typically take a shower. What did paying close attention to what you were doing do to the experience? Where else could you apply this?

I recommend you take a mindful shower each day this week, and in subsequent weeks you will be asked to select something else you currently do without much thinking and do it in a more mindful way as an informal practice to support your overall mindfulness practice.

Mindfulness and the Body

Another core mindfulness practice you'll be asked to start doing this week is the Body Scan meditation to practice noticing sensations of breathing and other sensations in the body, which is an easy way to make contact with the present moment. As you begin your mindfulness journey, you'll find that you can learn to bring attention to the body deliberately when you are being harassed by unhelpful internal chatter of the mind or are caught up in rumination about the future or past, and thereby regain your foothold back in the present moment. Similar to the breath, our body is with us at all times and can be an anchor to keep from being swept away by this chatter, so cultivating increased awareness of the body is also a foundational mindfulness exercise.

As I mentioned in Part I, mindfulness is an ability to keep attention on the present moment experience without getting too caught up in automatic thoughts and judgments. The second part of that description, "without getting too caught up in automatic thoughts and judgments," is something that also needs to be practiced to become a reality. Not only does the body scan help us learn to sustain our attention but also it enables us to practice bringing a curious and nonjudgmental attitude to bear on whatever experiences come our way. If judgment does come up automatically during the exercise, no problem. There's no need to chastise yourself. Just practice not getting caught up in the judgment further by judging the automatic judging that came up.

I recommend you do the Body Scan meditation each of the next 7 days. If you can't do it 7 days, do it 6; if you can't do it 6 days, do it 5. You get the point. Remember, the idea here is that if you do the practice, you see the results of the practice. These exercises, over time, actually "give back" much more than they take. If you feel you're too busy or that taking this type of "break" every day will negatively affect your performance, just think of these sessions the way elite athletes think of rest and recovery and mental conditioning. Every elite athlete knows that rest and recovery and mental conditioning are essential for peak performance. These exercises will sometimes seem like a break and other times seem like a workout; both experiences are beneficial.

The general flow of the body scan is quite simple. After taking a few moments to focus on the breath, you "scan" the body with the spotlight of attention, moving part by part in a systematic way and just noticing whatever sensations you find in each region of the body. Similar to the Awareness of Breath meditation, you will get lost in thought. When you do, just notice what you got caught up in and bring your attention back to where you had intended it to be within the meditation. Don't get too hung up on doing it perfectly. Be gentle with yourself and bring a sense of openness and curiosity to the experience.

You can read through the following meditation transcript and then do the exercise on your own without any guidance. However, especially if you are new to this, I recommend doing it as a guided meditation by listening to the audio files noted in the Resources, my teacher account on the Insight Timer app, or the resources section of http://www.clifsmith.com/; see Appendix page 189 for details. The audio guidance will help you stay on track until you are comfortable and/or interested in doing the exercise on your own.

Body Scan Meditation

Find a place to sit or lie down where you are least likely to be interrupted (although interruptions will happen from time to time). Similar to the Awareness of Breath meditation, the Body Scan meditation helps bring our minds into the present moment. Additionally, it strengthens our ability to notice physiological sensations of the body with more clarity. Physiological sensations can give early warning about the arrival of emotions. For example, anger may first show up as a heat on the back of the neck, gritting teeth, and shallow breathing. Although we may miss these sensations, they often arise before we're overtaken by the emotion they precede. If we become aware of those sensations as they arise, we may be able to stay present and respond more wisely instead of reacting automatically while lost in the strong emotion.

During the exercise we will be noticing what sensations are present in different regions of the body, whatever they are, and releasing any impulse to wish they were different from how we find them. Catching if we notice ourselves getting lost in judgment, self-criticism, or any other thoughts and stories, and coming back to the guidance in the meditation. Note that the goal here isn't to become relaxed, although that might happen. Instead we are just becoming present to what is here in this moment. Let's begin.

- ◆ Begin by taking a seated or lying down posture and settle in for the exercise. Once you're reasonably settled, allow the eyes to close if that's comfortable, and tune into your attention and awareness, just noticing whatever is here in the mind and body for a few moments. Allow whatever you notice to be just as it is and let go of any impulse to wish things to be different or wish them away.
- ◆ Hold the body with an attitude of unconditional friendliness and care.
- ◆ Become aware of the sensations of breathing.
- ◆ Notice the air as it enters the nose and causes the chest and abdomen to rise and as it makes its way back out of the body.

continued

- Release any impulse to control the breath, just noticing the process of breathing.
- And now guide the spotlight of attention down the left leg, into the left foot, and out to the toes of the left foot.
- Give full attention to the toes of the left foot and notice whatever sensations are present. Perhaps there is tingling. There may be warmth or coolness, some kind of temperature perception. There may be a lack of sensation; this is perfectly fine. We aren't trying to make any particular sensation happen; we are just noticing what's here.
- Now expand your attention to encompass the entire foot. The bottom, including the heel and sole, the top and sides of the foot. Explore any and all sensations. Bring a curious and nonjudgmental awareness to whatever you find here.
- Move attention into the ankle, an often-overlooked region of the body unless it's injured. What sensations are here now? If there are intense sensations associated with injury, notice them with that same curious and non-judgmental awareness.
- Continue now to move the spotlight of attention into the lower leg, calf, shin, sides of the lower leg, knee, and then the thigh, one after the other. Notice sensations in each of these regions of the body in turn.
- Acknowledge that, as we move attention into regions of the body, thoughts, emotions, memories, or other experiences associated with that region, such a knee injury or fall or other trauma may come up. If this happens, just allow those thoughts and emotions to arise and pass away on their own, recognizing they are merely thoughts. There is no need to push them away.
- And now guide the spotlight of attention down the right leg, into the right foot, and out to the toes of the right foot.
- Give full attention to the toes of the right foot and notice whatever sensations are present. Perhaps there is tingling. There may be warmth or coolness, some kind of temperature perception. There may be a lack of sensation; this is perfectly fine. We aren't trying to make any particular sensation happen; we are just noticing what's here.

◆ Now expand your attention to encompass the entire foot: the bottom including the heel and sole, the top and sides of the foot. Explore any and all sensations. Bring a curious and nonjudgmental awareness to whatever you find here.

◆ Move attention into the ankle to notice what sensations await you here.

◆ From time to time the mind may wander away from noticing sensations and get lost in thoughts, stories, anxieties, fantasies, worries, or regrets. When this happens, it's not a mistake. Just acknowledge what the mind was lost in and gently but firmly guide the attention back to where you had intended it to be.

◆ Continue now to move the spotlight of attention into the lower leg, calf, shin, sides of the lower leg, knee, and then the thigh, one after the other. Notice sensations in each of these regions of the body in turn.

◆ Release intentional awareness of the right leg and move the spotlight of attention into the hips and pelvis.

◆ The right hip. The left hip. And the entire pelvic region. Notice any sensations here.

◆ Shift attention now to the lower back, a place where we may carry tension, stress, and unpleasant sensations you might call "pain." If there are any of these types of sensations present, see if it's possible to just notice and let them be. Catch and Release any impulse to wish things were different than how you find them.

◆ Notice whatever sensations are present here, in this moment. Are they static? Do they change? Delve into the sensations to notice them as clearly as you can.

◆ Expand awareness to take in the middle and then upper back. Also include the back of the shoulders so that the entire back is on the main stage of awareness.

◆ Release awareness of the back and shift attention to the abdomen. Notice any sensations in this region of the body. Perhaps notice the movement of the breath here.

◆ Catch if you've become distracted or captivated by thoughts, stories, worries, desire to rush through the exercises, or boredom; acknowledge what the mind

continued

got lost in; and bring attention back to where you had intended it to be.

♦ Move attention from the abdomen to the chest. Notice sensations here, perhaps more clearly noticing the sensations of breathing, along with any other sensations that might be present. Sometimes subtle sensations are underneath more obvious ones.

♦ Shift attention now to take in both arms and hands. Bring a beginner's mind to this region of the body we know so well, and use every day. Notice the arms and hands as if for the first time and bring curiosity to whatever sensations are here.

♦ Let go of the arms and hands, moving attention into the shoulders and neck, which are also places we may hold stress and tension from time to time. What's true in this moment? Release any impulse to push away any unpleasant sensations but instead just notice what's here. Be open to and allow whatever is here to be fully felt.

♦ Release the shoulders and neck, bringing your attention now to the face and head, moving region by region beginning with the jaw, chin, mouth, nose, cheeks, temples, eyes, forehead, scalp, and back of the head. Notice any sensations along the way.

♦ And now expand the aperture of your attention wide like a floodlight so that your entire body is on the main stage of awareness. Notice the full landscape of sensations throughout the body.

♦ Now narrow the attention again and return it to the sensations of breathing for the last few moments of this exercise.

♦ I invite you to open your eyes if you've closed them and bring your attention back into the room you're in. Give yourself a moment to get your bearings before moving into the next part of your day.

After doing the Body Scan meditation for the first time you may have some questions. What does noticing sensations in the body actually do for us? How can doing that actually lead to any of the benefits ascribed to mindfulness? Some of these questions will be answered by you during this course, but in the interest of providing some insights I'll share a couple things. Increasing your awareness of sensations in the body helps us explore the difference between thinking about a sensation and experiencing it directly through our senses, which helps us discern between the thinking mind and sensing mind. It also trains us to observe sensations without over-analyzing or getting caught up in judgment, which has key crossover effects in other areas of our lives. Finally, a keener awareness of the body can act as an early warning system for incoming highly charged emotional reactions and can give you the space to make a shift from reaction to response. However, to read the messages the body sends, we must be able to pay clearer attention at a higher resolution to sensations that can arise from any part of the body and so we do the body scan to build that skill.

Key Points, Practices, and Signposts

Key Points

◆ We are on autopilot most of the time, living much of our lives lost in thought. Mindfulness helps us break this spell.

◆ Coming off autopilot enables us to be more fully engaged in all of our experiences, relationships, and activities. We can use the breath and the body as portals to the present moment because they are always with us.

◆ The Body Scan meditation increases our ability to notice increasingly subtle physiological sensations. This sensory acuity plays a major role providing advance warning of impending emotional states before we become overwhelmed by or lost in them.

Formal Practices

◆ Awareness of Breath meditation—twice a day for at least 10 to 15 minutes per session. (Chapter 6, page 58 or http://www.clifsmith.com)

◆ Body Scan meditation—once a day for 7 days. (this chapter, page 89 or http://www.clifsmith.com)

continued

Informal Practices

♦ Take a mindful shower—every day. (Appendix page 192)
♦ Catch and Release—Catch and Release one unhelpful internal belief, judgment, or thought each day. (Appendix page 191)
♦ S.T.O.P. practice—as needed. (Appendix page 192)

Signposts

♦ You may begin to notice your mind is "chattier" than you thought and how little control you have over your attention.
♦ You may begin to notice you experience previously overlooked moments a bit more vividly and to deliberately engage more fully with them.

Chapter 10

Week 2: The Mindset You Bring to Your Experience Matters

The quality of the mind determines the quality of the life. In this chapter we will explore important attitudes to bring to bear on our mindfulness journey and two modes of mind we bring to every situation: doing and being. We'll also touch on some common themes, challenges, and questions that come up when we first begin practicing mindfulness. But let's first start with a short story about two brothers, Allen and Sam, and how they show up in their lives.

Allen and Sam both grew up in New Orleans, Louisiana, in a stable middle-class family. Allen is a carpenter and Sam is a consultant. They've both worked themselves through school and have lives many people would envy: they both own homes, have good jobs in senior positions, and have no money troubles. They are successful by all objective measures. However, if you were to meet them face-to-face and have a conversation, you'd immediately realize there is a major difference in their experience of life.

Allen is quite easygoing. He's open to what life brings him because he believes there's a lesson to be learned in any situation. Even when faced with setbacks, Allen trusts that he can get through it. One of his favorite sayings is, "Well, I've already made it this far." If you were to ask him what he's doing on the weekend, it's probably spending time with his large group of friends. When asked to describe Allen, his friends say, "I can be myself around him. Even if we disagree, Allen doesn't judge and criticize everything I say or do. He accepts me for me."

Allen loves being a carpenter. As he puts it, "I get to work with smart people and solve challenging problems for clients with very specific tastes and always need to look at the project with fresh eyes so I can see all the possibilities. It's rewarding to complete the toughest jobs." Of course, some of the jobs are very complex and client changes midway through a project can test Allen's patience as he strives to complete them on time. In these moments, he reminds himself that he's lucky to have such a great job and changes are a part of the process. He knows if he or his team cuts corners, such as not allowing the wood glue to fully dry in its own time before moving to the next step, it would create even more problems and lead to a low-quality product even if is it done on time. So, while waiting for the glue to dry, Allen eases up a bit, focuses on what he can control, and brainstorms with his team how to incorporate the new changes into the project. It's difficult to get on Allen's team because there's rarely an opening.

Sam, however, might be best described as a tightly wound-up rubber band, always stressed about something. He works diligently to make sure nothing bad ever happens to him or his things. Sam doesn't do well with setbacks. He often says, "I've worked so hard to achieve all this; I can't lose it." A scratch on his car and he'll be upset for weeks. Being passed over for a promotion and he'll likely change jobs. If you were to ask Sam what he's doing this weekend, it's probably not spending time with a large group of friends. You see, Sam holds onto grudges anytime he perceives he's been slighted in some way, and often a mere disagreement with him is enough to put Sam off.

Sam enjoys being a consultant; it pays really well. His consulting projects are complex but he's an expert and already knows what most of his clients need. He likes to say, "I've seen it all, so I can solve it all." On Sam's projects, setbacks or delays are unacceptable and should be avoided at all costs because this would mean he failed and he's not a failure. He believes anything can be fixed and completed on schedule, whether it's a client-requested change or delays on his team. He judges his coworkers and often complains about them taking too long to get things done. Sam knows he's not perfect, either, but strives to be, so when he does make a mistake he's just as hard on himself. His view is that if you aren't going 100 miles per hour, you might as well not go. "Get it done on time, no matter what," is a common mantra coming from Sam to his team. He doesn't have time for soft things such as empathy or kindness because, in Sam's mind, these are signs of weakness and would only delay project progress. Sam has trouble keeping people on his team and when asked about why, his response is, "They just don't have what it takes to succeed."

. . .

We all have an "Allen" or "Sam" in our personal or professional lives, perhaps many of them. It's easy to see from our vantage point here, the importance of the attitudes they bring to their lives. Their approach to their individual situations contributes to the quality of their own experience, as well as to the experience of those around them. Which one would you rather work for: Allen or Sam? Who do you think would be more resilient in the face of losing a job or losing their home in a hurricane? Whose attitudes would be more conducive to learning the practice of mindfulness? It seems clear and obvious that Allen's would be, yet the attitudes we often bring to bear when trying to learn something new are more Sam-like than Allen-like.

Allen's approach to his life and work display some of the "attitudinal foundations," as Jon Kabat-Zinn calls them, that help support and strengthen us on our journey to being more mindful.[1] The attitudes are nonjudging, patience, beginner's mind, trust, non-striving, acceptance, letting go and letting be, gratitude, and generosity.

These attitudes are not only beneficial for our mindfulness practice but also they can be invoked and brought into all areas of our lives: in situations with our families and loved ones at home, with our colleagues at work, and in our interactions with ourselves.

Nonjudging
If you've been doing your daily mindfulness practices, you've probably already begun to notice the mind is constantly judging our experience. I like this exercise; I don't like this exercise. I like this person; I don't like this person. This chair is too soft; this chair is too hard. This is a boring waste of time, this is interesting and productive. We have a conditioned habit of putting things, people, and experiences into one of three categories: positive, negative, or neutral. If something makes us feel good, then it's in the positive category, we like it, and want more of it. If something makes us feel bad, then it's in the negative category, we don't like it, and we want it to go away.

If something doesn't make us feel anything, it's in the neutral category and we often don't even notice it.

You might be thinking, "Hey, isn't being able to judge things a good thing?" It certainly is a good thing when we aren't imprisoned by our judgments; unfortunately, most of us are. Like Sam, we tend to judge early and often, and when we've done this enough times, the process becomes automatic and difficult to see happening. It's almost as if we can't see beyond our judgments and they lock us into unconscious beliefs that can limit us and cut ourselves off from seeing situations, people, and ourselves more clearly.

The arising of judgments in reaction to experience is as automatic as the blinking of your eye in response to something coming close to it. The idea that you can *actively* turn off something that automatically pops up on its own, like hiccups, is ridiculous. This is why my definition of mindfulness is that it is an ability to keep attention on present moment experience *without getting too caught up in* automatic thoughts and judgments. I don't want you walking way with the belief that to be mindful your thoughts and judgments must cease or that they will cease. This could not be further from the truth. Thoughts will still be there; judgments will still automatically arise. You can be mindful in the midst of a storm of thoughts and judgments.

The aim for you over these next 8 weeks and beyond is to simply notice the judgments when they come up and remind yourself that we are practicing not getting caught up in the judgments. Catch and Release. There's no need to respond to noticing a particular judgmental thought by internally commenting, "I'm not supposed to be judging myself! I suck at this! I'm never going to get it." That's just more judging.

Patience

"Patience is a virtue," is an overused phrase that happens to be 100% accurate. We are so used to getting answers to our questions in seconds, receiving same-day deliveries from Amazon, and being able to watch our favorite TV shows any time we want that waiting even 5 minutes for something is excruciating for many people.

Life has its own timing. Just like Allen knows the wood glue dries in its own time, flowers bloom when they are ready. Of course, you plant your flowers in good soil, you water them daily, and you make sure they get good sunlight, but in the end, the flowers bloom when they are ready. You don't get mad at and berate flowers if they haven't bloomed by a certain date; how helpful would that be anyway?

Take care to be patient with yourself when your practice does not go the way you think it should or if you've not noticed enough "progress." Be consistent in your practice (daily water), work to incorporate these attitudes into your life (enriching your soil), and bring deliberate mindful awareness to as many moments as you can (sunlight), and the benefits of mindfulness will bloom when they are ready.

Beginner's Mind

As we gain more mileage in life, we tend to feel as if we already know the plot of the story and begin to take things for granted. We've gained so much information we seem to lose the ability to see the world, people, and situations with fresh eyes and without our internal running commentary about them. This leads us to miss out on amazing experiences and opportunities right in front of our eyes.

In the working world, we often become "experts" like Sam and have a harder time seeing things from new perspectives because we've "seen this type of client before" and we bring our preconceived ideas, plans, and opinions into the client meeting. Of course, it's important to plan and consider what a client might need, but a beginner's mind can help us see things we might otherwise miss.

Cultivating a beginner's mind and being curious can help us uncover and be receptive to new possibilities in our personal and professional lives. It can enable us to see that we do not have to be stuck in past experiences that have shaped our expectations and turned them into stone; that was then and this is now. Each moment is unique, distinct, and contains within it new possibilities.

Trust

Trust in yourself and trust the process. You may come across an exercise that you do not feel ready for yet, by all means trust your intuition. In the gym, trying to lift a weight suggested by your new trainer that you know to be much too heavy for you could be disastrous. It's important to be open to the guidance of a teacher (or trainer), but you are the one doing the exercises and seeing the results for yourself. There is a line between challenging and overwhelming and only you can determine where that is for yourself. Please note, though, that challenging often masquerades as overwhelming to keep you in your comfort zone.

There is wisdom within you that mindfulness practice will help you access. You've had gut feelings before. Perhaps, an intuition that told you the person you were dating wasn't right for you or that you shouldn't take a particular job after the interview in which you met the person who would be your new boss. These practices will bring you closer to what drives your intuitions so you can begin to trust yourself in situations where you may have relinquished that responsibility to others so they could tell you what's "best." The call here is to trust yourself and take radical responsibility for the life you are living. Similar to Allen, you've already made it this far; trust that you can do this, too.

Non-striving

Have you ever noticed that nearly everything we do is to achieve something or is in service to some agenda? This "doing" mode of mind is always noticing discrepancies between your self-generated expectations and your present reality, how things are versus how they "should" be. This mode is useful in many contexts, such as when you are analyzing an investment or developing a project plan, but bringing the "doing" mode into your mindfulness practice is not helpful. In mindfulness, the call is to practice not having an agenda and tuning into whatever arises during your meditation without trying to change it.

We are not sitting down and meditating to achieve a special state or to reach specific goals. This may sound odd because I asked you previously to identify why you are taking this course and what you want to get out of it. The thing is, with mindfulness, striving hard to reach your mindfulness "goal" actually pushes it further away. Remember, recalling your overall goal for taking the course can help motivate you to do the practice but then set it down when you sit down to meditate. Note: some meditations do have specific goals, such as to increase the feelings of empathy or compassion. Those aren't mindfulness meditations, given that striving for a particular state is embedded within the meditation itself. However, I will introduce a couple of these meditations later in the course because strengthening certain traits such as empathy and compassion support more effective connection and communication with others.

Acceptance

We waste a great deal of time and energy denying reality and trying to force situations, experiences, and even people into being how we would like them to be. Acceptance, within the context of mindfulness practice, is a willingness to see things actually as they are right now whether we like them or not. If you have lower back pain in this moment, accept that you have lower back pain instead of trying to deny or push the pain away. If your mind is agitated during your meditation, accept that's how it is in that moment. Acceptance is turning toward our experience and seeing it for what it is in the present moment. You don't have to like it, agree with it, or be excited about it. If the moment is uncomfortable or painful, acceptance enables us to process the experience instead of avoiding it. If the moment is positive, acceptance enables us to experience it fully.

Acceptance is not passive resignation in the face of unhelpful, unhealthy, or unsafe behavior or situations. Acceptance enables you to see situations or behaviors (even your own) more clearly, honestly, and openly, and it's from that perspective that you can take action to make a change where change is possible. Allen's acceptance of client changes mid-project as part of doing business, and focusing on what he could do is a good example of accepting something even if he doesn't like or want it. Spending time denying, struggling against, or pushing away reality only serves to increase stress, tension, and frustration.

Letting Go and Letting Be

As you've been practicing, you might have begun to notice the mind lingers on some thoughts, feelings, and situations and wants to turn away from others. We tend to automatically push away unpleasant thoughts, feelings, and experiences and get attached to pleasant ones. This is absolutely normal and understandable but becomes problematic when the unpleasant situation is here to stay or the pleasant situation has gone. Think of the pain that might be associated with not being able to let go of a relationship that has ended, a professional sports career cut short due to injury, or a job lost due to "restructuring."

In our practice here, the call is to release the habit of privileging some experiences over others. If you have a pleasant experience while meditating and it begins to dissolve, let it go. If you have a chain of unpleasant thoughts or judgments, there's no need to fight them, try to push them away, or engage with them; just let them be.

There is another angle to letting go as well. What are you still holding onto that, if you let it go, would open you up to new possibilities and opportunities? Do you cling to a story about your ability to speak in public that protects you from potential ridicule? Do you hold onto a belief that you could never start your own business, which keeps you in your comfort zone? Do you hold onto an identity of victimhood so that you don't have to take responsibility for your life? What are you holding onto that is keeping you a smaller version of your true self? Letting go in our mindfulness practice has a crossover effect that can allow us to let go of things outside the practice that may have much more influence on our lives, performance, and well-being.

Gratitude and Generosity

What do you focus more on: what you have or what you lack? Most people tend to notice what they don't have but would like to have, in their lives, homes, and relationships, and they almost completely overlook what they already have.

What are the implications of focusing on what you lack? If you are only, or even just primarily, noticing what you don't have, how might that be affecting your state of mind, level of contentment, or happiness? What would the impact be of primarily noticing what you have? Would you feel more abundance and satisfaction? When we feel we are living a life of abundance, we are much more likely to be generous toward others. This turns into a virtuous spiral: gratitude generates feelings of abundance, leading to generosity, which creates strong bonds of connection with others, leading to even more things for which we can be grateful.

Although not a mindfulness practice, having an "attitude of gratitude" is a skill we will cultivate by doing a gratitude journal, and it has a very healthy return on investment.

■ ■ ■

When we invoke these attitudes, we are practicing in a way that leads to an ability to face anything life throws our way and enables us to fully engage in the totality of our experience. The word for this is "equanimity." It's an ability to remain balanced and steady regardless of the situations in which we find ourselves. Equanimity enables us to make wise decisions despite high-pressure situations. Our mind is balanced and therefore our response can be balanced. It enables us to keep a wider perspective whether we've just won the lottery or were just passed over for promotion. It's the ultimate embodiment of the famous saying, "This, too, shall pass."

Shifting from Doing to Non-Doing, aka Being

When describing the non-striving attitude, I briefly touched on the idea of a "doing" mode of mind; more needs to be said about this way of engaging with the world. The doing mode uses critical thinking to solve problems and tries to narrow the gap between how things are and how we would like them to be.[2] It automatically carries out this work by noticing and highlighting that gap and then judging, analyzing, calculating, and questioning how to solve the problem (narrow the gap).

It may seem strange to talk about shifting from a doing mode to a non-doing or being mode in a book that purports to unlock exceptional performance, leadership, and well-being. You've gotten to where you are in your career and life by getting things done and solving problems! Why would you stop now? It's not about stopping; it's about balance.

The doing mode of mind is the thinking mind, the storytelling mind, and the striving mind, all wrapped into one, and we are automatically in it nearly every waking moment. It has enabled us to solve challenging problems in the world, invent new innovative products, and brought us into our current technologically advanced era. It enables you to plan your day, calculate your taxes, set and achieve goals, and solve difficult problems for you or your clients. However, it's also the cause of a great deal of suffering for us, personally.

The doing mode of mind automatically notices and highlights the gap between its self-generated expectations and its current view of reality and it does this for *everything*, whether it makes sense or not. Highlighting the gap is like seeing only what you lack and not what you have. Imagine you're sitting on a beach at a nice resort and you are absolutely content and happy, nearly blissful even. Then you notice the resort waiter go over to the group next you and give them two free drinks "on the house." The doing mode of mind automatically kicks in, asking, "Why did they get free drinks? I should get free drinks, too. It's totally unacceptable that they got free drinks and I didn't." Fifteen seconds ago, things were amazing and you were absolutely content and enjoying your moment on the beach; now, not so much. What changed? The doing mode of mind created a new self-generated expectation that was immediately not being met and highlighted that gap for you to ruminate over for, perhaps, the rest of the day.

Furthermore, the doing mode even tries to "solve" our difficult emotions or any feelings of unhappiness or unpleasantness regardless of the proximate cause. Emotions, negative self-views, or unhappy memories can't be "solved," and so this leads the mind to judge, worry, self-criticize, blame, overthink, ruminate, obsess, and mental time travel (i.e., constantly thinking about the future when things will finally be "good" or stuck in the past where things used to be "good"). So, although the doing mode is very useful, it's also very harmful if left to run amok.

Being mode is mindfulness; it's being present with whatever arises (noticing, accepting, nonjudging, and letting be) without any immediate pressure to change the experience even if it is unpleasant and without clinging to it even if it is pleasant. Deliberately moving into non-doing or being mode during our meditation practice begins to develop an ability to uncouple ourselves from the reactive thinking of the mind. When we do this, we are beginning to cultivate the ability to refrain from being caught up in unhelpful automatic thinking. Being mode also enables us to notice when we are (or are not) meeting our experiences with the nine attitudes I've described, and if those attitudes are not in play, it is very likely we are in doing mode.

Common Themes, Challenges, and Questions

When starting any new endeavor—whether it's learning a new instrument, a new language, or a new job—there are always setbacks, questions, and confusions. Starting a mindfulness practice is no different and so here are some common themes, challenges, and questions that have come up in my live training courses after the first week or so of practice.

I found it difficult to get started and found no time to practice. It can be very difficult to get started. Don't be discouraged. This challenge has been experienced by many people who have picked up a mindfulness practice. Yet, home practice is the key to reaping any benefits at all from mindfulness. Acquiring knowledge about mindfulness through books, webinars, and apps is nearly (not totally) useless without the accompanying practice. The insights and true knowledge are gained from doing the exercises consistently.

If this occurs again this week, I invite you to bring curiosity to what other thoughts and feelings are present when you are thinking you don't have time to do the practices. Have you come across these thoughts before when you've concluded you haven't had time for other things? What was your original intention for the course? Can you bring that intention to mind the next time you start feeling you don't have time and see what happens? What attitudes described in this chapter could you bring to bear on this situation?

My mind would not stay still; it was like a puppy running after anything that caught its attention. I'm not good at this. This is also one of the most common experiences in a new mindfulness meditator. Remember, one of the biggest myths of mindfulness is the belief that the goal is to try to stop all thoughts. Stopping all thoughts is not the goal. It's freedom with thoughts not freedom from thoughts.

It's also important to let go of any expectation of how you think (or hope) a particular mindfulness practice session is "supposed" to go. Simply see what's real in that moment. In that moment your mind was racing. That's okay; the idea is that when you notice you are lost in thought, just begin again and come back to the breath or body (or whatever the meditation guidance calls for). If you get lost in thought 500, 5,000, or 50,000 times, it's fine, just begin again.

When I do the Body Scan meditation the pain in my lower back becomes much more vivid. I'm doing this to relieve my pain, not intensify it. When we sit down to meditate and begin to focus the mind inwardly, we begin to "see" our inner experiences more clearly. Mindfulness invites us to look more closely at our experience, in this case, of pain and see what else there is to see. Is the pain always there? Is it static or does it change? What is coming up along with the pain? Thoughts? Judgments?

We also spend much of our time trying to push unpleasant experiences, such as pain, away. This is an automatic reaction that is not always helpful. When you feel pain or an itch during your practice,

I invite you to sit with it for a few breaths, instead of automatically moving/scratching. If, after a few breaths, it remains overwhelming and you must move, do so deliberately and mindfully. We do this to practice being with discomfort when it's voluntary (during meditation) so that we are better able to be with and handle discomfort when it's involuntary (tragedy, setbacks, and failures); this is the essence of resilience.

I find I fall asleep almost every time I try to meditate! Well, according to the CDC, more than 35% of all adults in the US aren't getting enough sleep, so maybe you're just tired.[3] I've found that the 3-minute meditation I do during my keynotes and classes is often the first time in weeks that many of my audience members have taken a pause from being "always on." This seems to be the norm in Western culture and so, when we step off the hamster wheel for a brief moment, we fall asleep. My first recommendation is to get more sleep, if that's possible. If not, here are a few things you can try to help you complete your meditation sessions. Similar to pain, see if you can just sit with sleepiness for a bit. Notice it arise and explore it with curiosity for a few moments, then, if you find you are still beginning to doze, you can just open your eyes slightly to let some light in. You also might try to incorporate your meditation into your morning routine after waking up and taking a shower. If you are lying down, you can try the meditation seated or even standing. Seated posture is important as well. If you are seated, be sure to sit up a bit more straight than normal and pull your back away from the chair; think, "relaxed yet alert."

Key Points, Practices, and Signposts

Key Points
- Mindset matters. Practice bringing the following attitudes into your practice and life: nonjudging, patience, beginner's mind, trust, non-striving, acceptance, letting go and letting be, gratitude, and generosity.
- Equanimity is an ability to remain balanced and steady regardless of the situations in which we find ourselves. We cultivate this during meditation, this letting go of hoping for or pulling in some experiences and pushing away others, so we can embody equanimity in our lives.

◆ Deliberately invoke the being mode when you notice the doing mode trying to solve a problem it's not designed to solve, such as a difficult emotion.

Formal Practices

These are the same as last week:

◆ Awareness of Breath meditation—twice a day for at least 10 to 15 minutes per session. (Chapter 6, page 58 or http://www.clifsmith.com)
◆ Body Scan meditation—once a day for 7 days. (Chapter 9, page 89 or http://www.clifsmith.com)

Informal Practices

◆ Mindful tooth brushing—every day. (Appendix page 192)
◆ Catch and Release—Catch and Release one unhelpful internal belief, judgment, or thought each day. (Appendix page 191)
◆ S.T.O.P. practice—as needed. (Appendix page 192)
◆ Gratitude journal—Before bed, write down one to three things you are grateful for from the day. What you are grateful for can be big (got a promotion) or small (had a refreshing glass of water).

Signposts

◆ You may begin to notice sensations in the body you have never been aware of previously.
◆ You may begin to recognize situations in which you are bringing the opposite of the nine attitudes in this chapter to situations in your life, such as judging, impatience, seen it all, distrust, striving, denial, grasping. Alternatively, you may notice situations in which you are surprised you were bringing one of the nine attitudes to a situation or situations in which you previously would have reacted to differently.

Chapter 11

Week 3: Do You Have the Story or Does the Story Have You?

Humans are storytellers. Just like children learn to speak far earlier than they learn to write, humans were telling stories long before the Sumerians began writing in cuneiform on clay tablets. If speaking comes before writing, what comes before speaking? Thinking, also known as the stories that occur inside our head. We've been telling ourselves stories for a very long time, and we are exceedingly good at it—so good, in fact, that we often don't even realize when we are doing it or how it affects us. This week we'll explore the power our stories and thoughts have in shaping our reality. Before we dive into the key learnings, let's hear about Alice, a senior manager on the path to partner at a Big Four accounting firm.

Alice has been at her firm for 12 years and "knows" this is *her* year to make partner. She's been consistently managing annual revenue in the $4 to $6 million range for the last 2 years and her sales pipeline for the next 4 years is pointing to continued revenue growth, so her business case for promotion is solid. She has good relationships with her peers and support for her partner candidacy across her business unit and with executive leadership in her service line. However, last week, during a pitch to a very important client, Alice made a blunder. Shortly after the presentation began, she called the primary client, the company CEO, by the wrong name. Alice, unaware of the gaff, continued with her presentation and, when she finished, the CEO said, "It all sounds great, we have a couple things to discuss internally and we'll get back to you. By the way, my name is Reggie not Carl." Alice, mortified, apologized profusely and left the meeting deflated.

As she left the meeting and headed back to her office to debrief with the team how the pitch went, she was thinking, "I'm such an idiot. My boss saw that mistake and the look on her face when Reggie mentioned it was pure disappointment. I'll be lucky if I have a job tomorrow."

Back in the office, as she approached the debriefing meeting room, Alice heard two people talking in hushed tones. They immediately stopped talking when she entered the room. It was her boss, Sarah, and the partner in charge of the client account, Bill, both of whom were in the pitch meeting. Alice immediately thought, "Oh, great, they are already talking about how I messed this up." She said, "Hi, I'm so sorry about what happened." Sarah and Bill both quickly responded that it was a mistake, but it's not a fatal one, and added that she still delivered a solid pitch. Alice nodded and responded, "okay," but immediately thought, "Oh, great, they won't even be honest with me about how much I ruined the entire pitch. What am I going to do?!" The debrief went as most do with the team walking away with lessons on how to do it better next time.

That night and for the next couple weeks, Alice could not sleep. She continued to ruminate about how badly she messed up and how she knew she was not going to make partner. Alice thought, "I cannot believe Sarah would be so petty as to prevent me from making partner over such a small mistake." The situation began to affect how Alice interacted with colleagues and Sarah in meetings. She became short with them, highlighting small mistakes they made, and was less collaborative with her peers across the business unit. On two more occasions, Alice came into a meeting room and Sarah and Bill stopped their conversation as soon as they saw Alice, further proving to her that her partner candidacy was sunk.

Alice's uncollaborative behaviors became more noticeable to her boss, who arranged for a one-on-one discussion about her performance the previous month. As soon as Alice received the meeting request, she could not help but think, "This is it, this is where she fires me, and for what? A small mistake with one client?! Well I'm not going to let them get rid of me on their terms, I'll quit first." The very next day Alice drafted her resignation to have it ready for the meeting with her boss.

In the meeting Sarah asked, "How have you been doing? I've noticed some changes in your behavior that seem to be affecting your performance, our relationship, and your relationship with the entire team." Her boss continued, "You've been doing so well here but in just the last 3 weeks, I've seen a side of you I haven't seen before and, I must be honest, it makes me hesitate to support your promotion. What's going on?"

Alice replied, "Well, ever since I made that mistake calling the CEO by the wrong name, I could tell you were extremely disappointed and had almost immediately made the call that I should not make partner. Which really upset me since I've dedicated so much to this firm and it was such a minor mistake. Plus, I can tell you and Bill both are on the same sheet of music, what with all the talking and immediately stopping every time I come in the room and so, why should I even try any more if all my hard work is gone over one mistake."

Sarah responded flatly, "Alice, we've just completed the fiscal year and Bill and I are having regular discussions about promotions and salary increases for our people, both of which are highly sensitive topics. We stop talking about those things when *anyone* walks in the room. After the meeting with the CEO, Bill and I both told you, although it was unfortunate you made that mistake, you still delivered a solid pitch. Your promotion was never in jeopardy over that small slip up but it is now due to the abrupt change in your behavior, which everyone, including me, Bill, and the entire team, have noticed."

Alice, stunned, said, "I'm sorry. I'm so sorry. I just thought . . ."

■ ■ ■

Rereading that story makes me cringe. I feel such a pang of sadness for Alice. She was miserable for a month and may have missed out on a promotion because she was caught in a story and that story had nothing to do with reality. Let me be clear here; this story applies equally to men, too. "Alice" could easily be "William" and be in the same situation. How does this happen? It happens because our minds are master storytellers and just like we can lose ourselves in a good movie, we get lost in our own story and fail to realize it's fiction or merely "based on a true story."

"Based on a true story" is apt here because it acknowledges that something happened but the producers of the movie changed the facts and circumstances for dramatic effect. In much the same way, an interaction or event happens in the world and you begin to make meaning, add significance, interpret, and narrate a story that is "based" on what happened but it is not reality. This is exactly why you and I can witness the same event and have a very different story about what happened. Unfortunately, we don't have that "based on a true story" disclaimer to remind us that our internal thoughts and stories aren't facts, and so we take our version to be the absolute truth or reality.

The process at work here can be described with the situation-interpretation–reaction model as seen in Figure 11.1. The situation is the actual event that unfolded. The interpretation is the meaning making that happens automatically and unconsciously by the mind, and it comes in the form of thinking, assuming, ascribing intent to

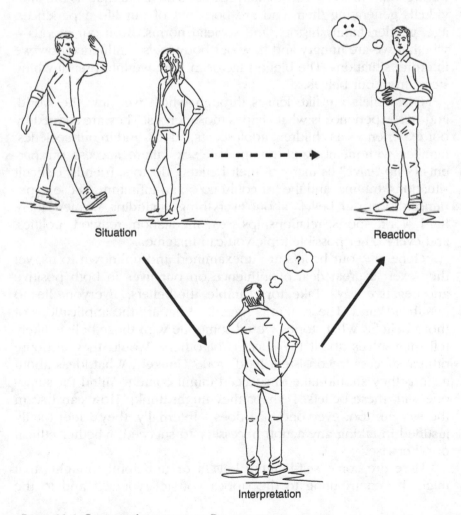

Situation

Reaction

Interpretation

FIGURE 11.1 SITUATION–INTERPRETATION–REACTION MODEL.

Source: From 99designs.com/Konstantin. Reprinted with permissions of 99designs.com.

others' behaviors, "mind reading," storytelling, and judging. The reaction includes our emotional reactions, the options we feel we have, the impulses to action we feel we should take, our automatic responses, and so on. We erroneously think we are reacting to the situation, but in fact we are reacting to our interpretation. We aren't seeing the world as it is; we are seeing it as we are.

If you recall in Chapter 4, we saw this process play out in the scenario in which someone walks by and doesn't acknowledge your greeting. Our automatic interpretation process comes online. We interpret every single interaction, event, and experience nonstop throughout our lives. Those interpretations are as unique as the individuals generating them and are born out of our life experiences, age, gender, family history, and societal norms. Even our moods—whether we are hungry and how our body feels—influence how we interpret situations. The biggest factor in how we interpret anything stems from our beliefs.

Our beliefs are like lenses through which we view the world, and our experience is what shapes those lenses. They are shaped by our experiences as children, adolescents, adults, and in our societies, families, with members of the opposite sex, failure, success, our parents (who "gave" us many of their beliefs), doctors, friends, difficult situations, trauma, and the list could go on ad infinitum. These experiences form our beliefs about everything, including women, men, hard work, sports, relationships, sex, meditation, religion, politics, and every other possible topic you can imagine.

Generally, our beliefs are unexamined and unknown to us, yet they exert a great deal of influence on our lives in both positive and negative ways. Take, for example, the beliefs, "Everyone lies to get ahead" and "The system is rigged." What are the implications of those beliefs? What stories would someone with those beliefs likely tell themselves about the success of others? Would they attribute others' success to consistent hard work? Unlikely. What ideas about actions they should take to succeed might come to mind for someone with these beliefs? Perhaps they might think, "How can I scam the system, too; everyone else does?" Internally, they'd feel totally justified in taking any action necessary to succeed, whether ethical or otherwise.

Here are some self-limiting beliefs or unhelpful thoughts that might be contributing to the stories you tell yourself and to the pressure, stress, anxiety, disappointment, or anger you might feel in reaction to particular situations:

- ◆ If I make a mistake, I'm a failure.
- ◆ No one in their right mind would love me.
- ◆ I could never speak in front of a crowd of people.
- ◆ Nothing is ever my fault.
- ◆ Everyone is competition.
- ◆ If people don't believe what I believe, they are bad people.
- ◆ Everyone leaves me in the end.
- ◆ I don't belong.
- ◆ I'm bad at finance.
- ◆ I'll never be able to learn this.
- ◆ I always have to fix things.
- ◆ If I want it done right, I have to do it myself.
- ◆ If I don't do it, it won't get done.

The point here isn't to change our thoughts, beliefs, or stories into "better" ones. Instead, the aim is to begin to recognize that thoughts, beliefs, and stories are not facts. They can be true, partially true, or absolutely false. As we recognize this, thoughts, beliefs, and stories have less power over us, we learn we don't have to act on them, and we begin to notice that the stories we tell ourselves are what create our experience of life, our individual "reality." The theme, tenor, and tone of the stories you tell yourself (and buy into) are the theme, tenor, and tone of your experience.

Mindfulness of Sounds, Thoughts, and Emotions

In Part I, I described two types of mindfulness-building exercises: focused attention and open awareness meditations. We will now begin to expand beyond the breath and body as objects of our meditation and begin to include more objects to bring our awareness to during meditation. We transition from focusing on one object of meditation (breath) to becoming aware of more objects as they enter and leave our field of awareness.

An example of this is doing an open awareness meditation that uses sounds in your environment as the objects of the meditation.

In this type of meditation, you just notice the arising and passing away of any sounds that happen to come to your attention and awareness. For example, you might hear the humming of your laptop fan, then notice the din of traffic outside your window, then the sound of a lawn mower, and so on. You would not privilege any particular sound; instead, just receive any sound that happens to arise, notice it and even notice the silence between sounds. You can do the same with thoughts and emotions as objects of awareness, and, eventually, you can sit and just notice the arising and passing away of anything and everything in your awareness. The Mindfulness of Sounds, Thoughts, and Emotions meditation[1] is one such open awareness meditation.

You can read through the following meditation transcript and then do the exercise on your own without any guidance. However, especially if you are new to this, I recommend doing it as a guided meditation by listening to the audio files noted in the Resources, my teacher account on the Insight Timer app, or at http://www.clifsmith. com; see Appendix page 189 for details. The audio guidance will help you stay on track until you are comfortable and/or interested in doing the exercise on your own.

Sounds, Thoughts, and Emotions Meditation

The Sounds, Thoughts, and Emotions meditation is an open awareness meditation. We will be widening the aperture of our awareness beyond just focusing on the breath and allow for a broader focus on the landscape of sounds, thoughts, and emotions. This helps us see the similarities among sounds, thoughts, and emotions. They arise on their own, whether we want them to or not. They can hijack our attention and captivate us. And we can also come to realize that it's possible to view them as events that merely enter and exit our awareness, thus gradually lessening our habitual reactivity to them. Let's begin.

♦ Sit up in the chair or whatever is supporting the body and allow both feet to be flat on the floor. Allow the eyes to close, if that feels comfortable, or soften the gaze and angle it down toward the floor. Begin by noticing the sensations of breathing where you feel them most prominently, just as you've been doing in the Awareness of Breath meditation.

♦ Release any impulse to control the breath; just allow the body to breath on its own.

♦ Reasonably settled, allow awareness now to expand and encompass in the entire body. Notice the full landscape of the body in awareness, including the sensations of breathing but do not solely focus on the breath. Merely open to a fuller awareness of what's being experienced in this moment.

♦ Allow sounds now to take the main stage of awareness. Of course, other things may be in your awareness but tune into the sounds specifically. Notice sounds behind, in front, beside, above, or below you.

♦ Catch any automatic tendency to hear and immediately name the sounds heard, such as that's a fan, car door, music, lawn mower, or kids playing. Notice any automatic judgments, stories, or other reactions that praise or push away the reality that these sounds are here in this moment. If this happens, tune back into the sounds themselves and explore the possibility of letting them be.

♦ When focused on our breathing we sometimes notice the small gaps between breaths, when there's neither in- nor outbreath. Perhaps you can become aware of the space between sounds.

♦ Move now from tuning into sounds to becoming more broadly aware of any thoughts arising in the mind, perhaps thoughts about the exercise, boredom, or about your to-do list, or maybe worries or frustrations. Experiment with witnessing thoughts arising into your awareness, lingering a while, and then dissolving.

♦ Not trying to make thoughts happen, just notice, like sounds, thoughts come and go on their own within the mind.

♦ When thoughts arise in the mind, see them floating by like clouds passing across an otherwise clear sky. Your mind is like the sky; your thoughts are like the clouds—sometimes large, sometimes small, sometimes dark,

continued

sometimes light—but the sky remains. The sky does not prefer some clouds over others.

♦ Whatever thoughts there are, try to see them as mental events that are arising in the mind, lingering, and then dissolving.

♦ You may find, after a while, that you get captivated by your thinking, no longer observing thoughts but caught inside them. When this happens, it's not a mistake. Just acknowledge what the mind got caught in and begin again. Notice these mental events as they arise, linger a while, and then pass away.

♦ Bring awareness to any emotions that may be present as well. Notice the arising and passing away of emotions in your awareness.

♦ Anytime the mind gets caught up in thoughts, stories, or emotions it's always possible to come back to the breath to stabilize awareness in the present moment before beginning again and focusing on the coming and going of thoughts and emotions.

♦ Come back to focus on the sensations of breathing for the last few moments of this exercise.

♦ And remember that the breath is always available, in any situation, to help bring you back into the present moment and to a state of mindful awareness.

♦ I invite you to open your eyes if you've closed them and bring your attention back into the room you're in. Give yourself a moment to get your bearings before moving into the next part of your day.

Doing this type of open awareness meditation builds the ability to not be taken in by the stories created by the mind and yields a number of insights into the nature and habits of our minds and patterns of thinking. We can see through this meditation that we have just about as much control over what thoughts and emotions arise as we do over what sounds arise. The fact that you can "sit back" and notice thoughts arise and pass away, while you're still "here," is a clue that you are not your thoughts and you don't have to let them control you. With consistent practice, we can begin to notice our thoughts and emotions without getting caught inside them—seeing them at a distance so to speak. This leads to a freedom that unlocks our innate ability to respond to life instead of reacting automatically based on a distorted view of reality.

Common Themes, Challenges, and Questions

I'm finding when I do my basic Awareness of Breath meditations, I'm not getting relaxed. This seems like a waste of time if it's not a break. Remember, the purpose of mindfulness meditation is not to become relaxed, although that is a nice "side effect" that often shows up in response to our practice. These formal mindfulness meditations aren't breaks designed to relax us; they are mental workouts designed to increase our baseline level of mindfulness. Sometimes workouts make us feel energized and refreshed. Sometimes they make us feel uncomfortable and challenged (like when I do squats!). In both cases, they benefit our fitness level. It's the same with mindfulness meditations. Some sessions will feel "easy" and others will feel "difficult," but both are beneficial. Our purpose with mindfulness is to be able to meet each moment of our lives fully, without getting too caught up in our automatic thoughts and judgments. This frees us from being caught in the tyranny of constant rumination and unhelpful and disempowering stories. Then, when we take a break, it's actually a break and not just another moment where we are ruminating or criticizing ourselves about what's still on our to-do list, what more productive things we "should" be doing, or for needing a break in the first place.

My mind continues to get lost in thought during my meditations. I've been doing this for 2 weeks now; shouldn't I be better? Notice that even in a meditation we can be caught in the "doing" mode of mind, trying to achieve a certain "level" or be the "best" meditator. If, each time you notice you are lost in thought, you acknowledge what your mind got caught in and come back to the meditation, you are doing the exercise the way it's intended to be done. Try to allow your experience to be whatever it is and endeavor to bring in the attitudes we discussed previously (nonjudging, patience, beginner's mind, trust, non-striving, acceptance, letting go and letting be, gratitude, and generosity) into your practice and life in order to aid with this.

You say that thoughts aren't facts and getting caught up in our thinking is something we should avoid. How am I supposed to do my job and analyze situations and make good decisions? I get paid to make interpretations and provide my opinion on situations. Let me first say that mindfulness isn't the enemy of thinking; it's the enemy of thinking without knowing you're thinking. That's a big distinction. When we are lost in thought, we are experiencing and reacting to thought, not reality. It's okay to deliberately think, plan, and analyze; those are key aspects of being a productive member of society. Even then, though, if we are unaware of the filters (beliefs) we have that delete, distort, and generalize reality, we might be missing important perspectives. Not knowing you are locked into an unhelpful or self-limiting belief can result in continuously sabotaging relationships, keeping you small, and missing out on opportunities right in front of you. Lack of awareness of these things results in not having a choice at all. Once a previously unconscious pattern of thinking or belief moves into our conscious awareness, we are able to make a choice. Because, once you become aware of something, you can do something about it or not do something about it. Perhaps ask yourself, "Does this way of thinking or belief serve me?" For example, if through your practice you uncover that you have some of the following beliefs and the answer to whether they are serving you or not is "yes," then by all means keep them:

- If it's possible to do, I can do it, too.
- I can handle what life throws at me.
- I control my actions, not my outcomes.
- I am worthy of love, just as I am.
- My decisions matter more than my circumstances.
- Nothing is permanent.
- There is something to learn in every setback.
- Every day is a gift and a chance to start fresh.
- The past is in the past; it doesn't define me.
- The pain of regret is worse than the pain of failure.

Key Points, Practices, and Signposts

Key Points

- Our thoughts, beliefs, and stories are not facts or reality. They can be true, partially true, or totally false.
- Situations are interpreted differently by each individual. Everyone's story is "based on a true story," but no one has the "true story." Remember, you are reacting to your interpretation of the situation instead of the situation itself.
- The fact that you can observe your thoughts gives you the ability to make a choice about whether you are going to act on them or not.

Formal Practices

- Awareness of Breath meditation—twice a day for at least 10 to 15 minutes per session. (Chapter 6, page 58 or http://www.clifsmith.com)
- Mindfulness of sounds, thoughts, and emotions—once a day for 7 days. (This chapter, page 114 or http://www .clifsmith.com)

Informal Practices

- Mindful tea/coffee drinking—every day. (Appendix page 191)
- Catch and Release—Catch and Release one unhelpful internal belief, judgment, or thought each day. (Appendix page 191)
- S.T.O.P. practice—as needed. (Appendix page 192)
- Gratitude journal—before bed, write down one to three things you are grateful for from the day. What you are grateful for can be big or small.

Signposts

- You may begin to catch yourself lost in unhelpful thoughts, beliefs, or interpretations.
- You may begin to recognize situations in which you automatically believe the internal story but then pause and ask, "Is this really true? What lenses am I looking through? What is actually happening right now?"

continued

◆ You may begin to notice that thoughts and emotions, like sounds, arise of their own accord and eventually dissipate. You might become aware that you can "look" at thoughts and emotions in the same way, just noticing them and not getting involved with them.

Chapter 12

Week 4: The Saber-Toothed Tiger of the Modern World: Everything

"If I had 8 hours to chop down a tree, I'd spend 6 sharpening my axe" is a quote attributed to Abraham Lincoln. I've seen variations on the number of hours noted in this quote, but the point is true: preparing and maintaining one's tools is just as, if not more, important than the task itself. We've spent the first three sessions preparing for the next two and beyond. Our version of sharpening the axe has been sharpening our attention, increasing our awareness of bodily sensations, and being able to see thoughts and emotions as mental events. Keeping those mental tools sharp is a continuous process, and the exercises you've learned thus far are fundamental mindfulness practices and important to revisit regularly.

Now we will begin to use that increased focus, sensory clarity, and insight to explore how we relate to the challenges and difficulties we face in our daily lives. Let's first listen in on a conversation over coffee on a Saturday morning between Mitch and Tamika about Mitch's upcoming presentation at his company's annual training week.

"Did I tell you my boss asked me to present our new marketing strategy at our big annual training week?" Mitch wondered aloud.

"No! Congratulations! What an amazing opportunity!"

"Yeah, an amazing opportunity to embarrass myself in front of 300 people, including the board," Mitch whispered almost inaudibly.

"What? C'mon, you'll be great up there. You know your stuff."

"I know I know my stuff. I've been practicing every day and really hope I do it perfectly, but just the thought of going up there makes my stomach turn. I haven't been able to sleep and I'm afraid of what will happen if I bomb it, which I probably will."

"Didn't you just tell me the other day you did a great job presenting the budget numbers two weeks ago? You even said, 'My boss told me I was articulate and effective.'"

"*That* was a presentation to six people, and it was just budget numbers. This is much different. I'll be on stage. I might trip walking up there and then everyone will be laughing at me or worse, pitying me. What if the slides won't load and I have to try to present the strategy without them and I get things wrong? People will think I'm incompetent. I just can't stand it. Even now my heart is racing, my palms are sweaty, and my stomach is doing flips."

"Okay, so it is a bigger deal, but you can practice on me. I'd be happy to be your guinea pig. How much time do we have until you make your big Broadway"—raising and spreading her arms wide in exaggeration—"debut?" Tamika offers, trying to lighten the mood.

"Two months."

■ ■ ■

As complex as we humans are, we have some very basic reactions to life. We tend to go through life bouncing between seeking or clinging to pleasure and avoiding or pushing away pain. This makes sense, of course. We typically desire experiences that are pleasurable and are averse to ones that are unpleasant; we want success rather than failure, gain rather than loss, and praise rather than criticism. However, as the Rolling Stones sang in 1969, "You can't always get what you want."

We know, intellectually, we can't always get everything we want, but we still tend to get fixated on and cling strongly to the pleasure side, which sets us up for even more suffering when things inevitably change. When we make the mistake of believing that our happiness and well-being are dependent on getting or keeping the pleasurable things we desire, the pain of not getting or losing those things is all the greater.

This also creates a sense of wishing and hoping for things to be a certain way and/or fearing what we don't want to happen will happen. These hopes and fears can begin to dominate our thinking and create stress and anxiety for us, even when everything is fine. This is what is happening to Mitch in the chapter-opening story. We know he is having coffee with a friend on a Saturday and yet he is consumed by stress and anxiety about something that is *two months* away! We even know it's been affecting his sleep. The purpose of mindfulness is to stay in the present moment and let go of the tendency to grasp at what is pleasant and push away what is unpleasant.

Can you relate to Mitch's story, stressing over something that isn't happening right now and may never happen quite the way he imagines it? When we do this, we are not only missing out on what might be a pleasurable experience in the present moment but also we feel real stress about a situation that may never come to pass. Even if the stressful situation is definitely going to happen, what is the value of feeling the "pain" or stress of it more than once? This imbalanced equation, in which we experience the stress of one moment many times before and after it happens, is one of the reasons chronic stress is at epidemic levels in our society. Chronic stress is a major contributing factor to the six leading causes of death in the United States: cancer, coronary heart disease, accidental injuries, respiratory disorders, cirrhosis of the liver, and suicide.[1]

Stress and Our Stress Response

What is stress and is it always bad? There are many very technical definitions of stress in medical journals and books but basically, **stress is your body's way of responding to threats, demands, or pressures placed on it, whether real or perceived.** Stress is not always bad. In fact, it can be quite helpful. At the right level—and it is a different level for everyone—stress can help us perform at our best. However, too much stress at once or sustained moderate to high levels of stress over a long period of time, known as "chronic stress," can wreak havoc on our body and mind. Let's break it down a bit.

When faced with a threat, the stress response (also known as the "fight-or-flight" response) kicks into gear, and the hypothalamus sends an alarm signal, which releases hormones, including cortisol and adrenaline.[2] This leads to a cascade of other effects that boost our energy and strength, such as increasing sugar in the bloodstream, shutting down "nonessential" systems, and increasing the heart rate, blood pressure, and breathing rate. Pupils dilate and oxygen uptake further increases as your bronchial tubes and other airways in the lungs dilate, which brings us into a heightened state of focus. Depending on the type of threat and our automatic appraisal of it, we either fight or flee. All of this is designed to enhance our chances of survival, and it has worked very well for us or we wouldn't be here to know about it. Now understanding this, let's turn our attention back to how it affects us today.

What are some things that cause stress in your life? I ask that question in all my courses and the answers come flooding in: deadlines, workload, unbearable bosses, job interviews, first day of work, "helpful" transformations at work, last day of work, getting laid off, retirement, wedding planning, marriage, my husband, my wife, my kids, my in-laws, separation, divorce, finances, traffic, arguments, holidays, news, social media, cancel culture, tax season, talking to the opposite sex, talking to anyone, politics, talking to Democrats, talking to Republicans, buying a home, remodeling a home, selling a home, change, having to hear about mindfulness all the time, and the list goes on and on. Notice that some stressors are "good," such as getting a job interview or first day of work, and some are "bad," such as losing a job. Also, what's not on this list? Saber-toothed tigers! Why? Well, they are extinct so that's one reason, but snakes, bears, and non-extinct tigers aren't on the list, either, because we are doing so well as a species that, for most of us, most of the time, our lives are not in real physical danger.

What commonly triggers our stress response has changed over the course of modern civilization, but our response system has changed very little. When the situation triggering our stress response involves real physical danger (i.e., a snake, speeding car, or tiger), it can help us survive by enabling us to act immediately and powerfully. However, if the stress response is coming online in reaction to non-dangerous "threats" (e.g., public speaking, criticism, or someone disagreeing with us), we feel tense, anxious, and aggravated because there is no outlet for the extra energy coursing through our body.

One of the most powerful abilities we have as humans is our ability to simulate situations in the mind. We can remember the past, anticipate the future, and plan a course of action. This ability brought us to the top of the food chain and has been used by athletes, elite special forces operators, and intelligence officers for decades to visualize (and realize) exceptional performance under pressure. However, in the untrained mind, we can get completely taken in by a simulation or story of a potential stressful situation, and our brain and body will respond in the same way as if it were happening in the present moment. Adrenaline pumps, heart rate increases, emotions arise, and so on, just like in Mitch's situation. It's as if he is being attacked by the tiger 2 months before the tiger arrives.

In contrast to humans, when a group of antelope is faced with the very real threat of an attacking tiger, the process unfolds quite a bit differently. First, they probably weren't chewing on their little antelope hooves nervously a few weeks before facing the tiger. The threat appears in the present, the animals' stress response jumps into action, and they bound away en masse. The threat is avoided or perhaps one antelope is eaten. The stress levels of those not eaten recovers to baseline a short while later. They are soon back to grazing and definitely aren't ruminating for weeks about the tiger that had the audacity to attack them that one time. Unfortunately, this does not happen for most people in the modern world. We perceive non-dangerous things as dangerous threats, then tend to pre-live (or relive) them. We get caught in negative thoughts, ruminations, and stories in our inner world, which trigger our brain in similar ways to actual danger in the outer world. This happens over and over again, and our stress response systems rarely fully recover before the next "threat" presents itself.

We then have a constant higher baseline level of stress, near continuous release of stress hormones, leading to the effects of chronic stress such as high blood pressure, inflammation, immune system suppression, headaches, insomnia, anxiety, pain, backaches, and so on. That's just stress's impact on the body. There's also lack of concentration, inability to focus, confusion, and brain fog that result from how chronic stress affects the mind. Finally, there's the relational impact of chronic stress; poor communication, short temper, withdrawal, detachment, lack of emotion or ability to show affection are all potential negative effects.

What are some unhelpful ways people try to cope with stress? This is also a question I ask in all my courses and the answers come flooding in: drinking wine, drinking beer, social media, retail therapy, working too much, eating, abusing legal drugs, illegal drug use, smoking, avoiding taking risks, taking excessive risks, suppressing emotions, and so on. When you take some of these behaviors to their logical conclusions, you experience results such as addiction and depression and eventually a systemic breakdown in the form of heart attacks, exhaustion, loss of motivation, and burnout.

You may be thinking, "The modern world is the way it is, and higher stress is just the new normal." Well, you're right; it is the new normal—for those who do not train their mind. We are not helpless, even when we don't control everything that happens to us.

What's the alternative? Of course, you can take a traditional stress management course, which will give you tips and tricks to be more efficient with your time, say "no" more effectively, or exercise more (all very helpful things by the way). However, what is often overlooked in those courses is that the source of much of our stress is not coming from the outer world but from the perceptions and stories we create in our inner world. And then there is that imbalanced equation I mentioned, when we have one actual stressful moment (in the past or *possibly* coming soon) that we relive or pre-live over and over again, adding stress where it could just be one and done.

As we continue to build our mindfulness "muscles" and learn that many of our automatic interpretations, assessments, and stories about past, present, or future situations are not true accounts of reality, our brain will begin to realize that speaking in front of a crowd, having a potential date turn us down, failing at something, receiving criticism, having someone disagree with us, making a mistake, and many other anticipations or situations that trigger our stress response, are not actually life-threatening situations. Then we can step out of our unhelpful cycle of self-generated stress production. Being able to discern between non-self-generated stress and self-generated stress is a superpower. Stress is a part of life; there's no question about that. Fortunately, when you reduce the amount of self-generated stress you create, you'll have more resources and wisdom to deal with the inevitable stresses in life that affect all of us by virtue of being human.

Fortunately, practicing mindfulness helps us with both types of stress; it helps us reduce self-generated stress and helps us cope more effectively with inevitable stress. Being able to pause in the midst of a stressful situation, catch our automatic reactions and release them so we can respond more thoughtfully, tends to result in less stress overall. This is particularly true as we see the process unfold successfully and our confidence in our own ability to face any challenge improves. As our confidence improves, we won't even see certain situations as stressful any longer because we will already know we can handle them.

Common Themes, Challenges, and Questions

My open awareness meditation practice has been much harder than the focused attention meditations. My mind is all over the place. Is this normal? Some people report that passively observing sounds, thoughts, and emotions is more difficult than doing a focused attention meditation or a body scan. The body scan is the first transition from having one object of meditation to more than one while still "anchoring" our focus in specific regions of the body in turn. The mind has a bit more "freedom," but we keep it on a specific track so to speak. In open awareness meditations, the mind has nothing to "do," and this can sometimes lead to agitation and increased chatter, judgment, and other distractions that take us in. This is a completely normal part of the process, and the call is always to come back to the intention of the exercise. Notice your reaction to the mind's behavior and how you meet it. Do you meet it nonjudgmentally and with patience?

I've been meditating for quite a while and things haven't changed. Let me clarify; I do feel better and I'm less stressed out, but my life hasn't changed. I still have the same overbearing boss and challenges with work in general. Am I just accepting a bad situation?

This is what I meant when I said that the quality of the mind determines the quality of the life. Mindfulness is not about having new and different kinds of experiences but to "see" our experience in a new way and respond from that place. This is the power of perception and of ceasing to automatically react to life in ways that exacerbate already challenging situations. Sometimes we can change our external circumstances (e.g., changing jobs) and sometimes we can't change them (e.g., we've already fallen and broken our leg), but we can always look at what we are bringing to the situation in terms of our own reaction or response. A similar thing can happen with arguments between spouses. You can have the same spouse and same disagreements but find you are having fewer and less intense arguments since picking up a mindfulness practice. A closer look as to what is happening between you and your spouse may reveal that it's not better because of something new you are doing but because of something you are *no longer* doing. Perhaps there is a letting go of a pattern of automatic reaction that typically turns a disagreement into a personal attack.

Are you saying all stress is in our heads? No, not *all* stress. I'm saying a great deal of stress is optional, because it is often caused by stories and/or misperceptions in the mind, as well as by anticipating and resisting an upcoming potentially stressful event or reliving one from the past. Stop buying into the stories and the optional stress won't survive it. There is the stress we will have because of a situation, such as giving a speech. However, we really don't need to have that stress over and over again by anticipating for 2 months everything that could go wrong in the speech or reliving that one time 4 months ago when the speech didn't go perfectly.

Key Points, Practices, and Signposts

Key Points

◆ It's totally normal to desire pleasurable experiences and be averse to unpleasant ones, but we tend to cling so strongly to getting what we want or avoiding what we don't want that our hopes and fears in this regard can begin to dominate our thinking and create stress, anxiety, and depression, even when everything is fine. Bring your mind to the present moment and let go of the tendency to grasp at what is pleasant and push away what is unpleasant.

◆ Stress is a natural part of our lives and can actually improve our performance, but we have a great deal of self-generated stress that we can be free of by becoming aware of what we are doing with our own minds. Catch when you are reliving or pre-living a stressful event to begin to step out of the cycle and move toward making stressful situations one and done.

Formal Practices

◆ Awareness of Breath meditation—twice a day for at least 10 to 15 minutes per session. (Chapter 6, page 58 or http://www.clifsmith.com)

◆ Mindfulness of sounds, thoughts, and emotions—once a day for 7 days. (Chapter 11, page 114 or http://www.clifsmith.com)

Informal Practices

- Mindful eating—every day. (Appendix page 191)
- Catch and Release—Catch and Release one unhelpful internal belief, judgment, or thought each day. (Appendix page 191)
- S.T.O.P. practice—as needed. (Appendix page 192)
- Gratitude journal—before bed, write down one to three things you are grateful for from the day. What you are grateful for can be big or small.

Signposts

- You might begin to realize, as you continue noticing thoughts, that many of them are repeats and self-referential (i.e., I, me, mine related).
- You may begin to notice "letting go" in your life and in situations when you previously reacted in the same way again and again.
- Internal chatter may become similar to the din of conversations in the background at a busy restaurant. Some words, comments, or conversations still draw you in, but not as many, with less intensity, and for a shorter period of time.

Chapter 13

Week 5: Delving into the Difficult

Congratulations on reaching the halfway point in the course! This is a good time to check in with your intention for picking up this book and taking this journey as well as to recognize how far you've come. Making it this far is already further than most people will ever go in service to understanding themselves and their minds with increased clarity.

We continue with the theme of looking at our relationship with difficulties that arise in our lives and begin to see how two people can respond very differently to setbacks, such as losing a job, getting sick, or losing a client. We will also take some concrete steps to delve into difficult situations in an effort to build our ability to grow from life's setbacks and misfortunes to be able to flex to rapidly changing situations and to maintain poise and presence of mind in the midst of high-pressure situations, which are invaluable skills in today's modern world. Before we dive in, let's first look at some setbacks and challenges people have been facing recently.

In the US, as I write this chapter, about 40 million people have lost their jobs in the last 90 days due to the economic impacts of the COVID-19 pandemic. Not only have people lost jobs but also millions more have been infected with the coronavirus or have loved ones fighting, recovering, or who have died from the disease. Some have lost their jobs *and* are having the disease affect them and/or their family members. The challenges people are facing in this moment are only matched by the uncertainty of what's next.

Anyone watching the news during the first 6 months of the COVID-19 pandemic was seeing or hearing things about COVID-19 infected/death numbers continuing to rise; states opening, states reclosing; there's no need to wear a mask; wait, everyone should wear a mask; COVID-19 is only affecting the elderly and people with underlying conditions; actually, it's also dangerous for children and people in their 20s, 30s, 40s, and 50s; we've got a handle on it; we don't have a handle on it; schools are opening in the fall; schools will be closed; schools will be open but only for some kids . . .

Given this situation, it's quite easy to see how people could slip into an unhelpful spiral of increasingly negative rumination and further amplify their own stress, fear, anxiety, and even depression. In fact, many people are already in that spiral and some of them will not recover. And yet, similar to all previous tragic, challenging, and even horrific times, inspiring stories of courage and comeback will inevitably emerge.

We will eventually hear about a woman who quit her job in January 2020, got a business loan to start a restaurant, and lost it all due to COVID-19 business closures in April 2020, but then bounced back and took it further by creating one of the most successful online bakeries. We'll also hear about someone just like her, with similar circumstances, background, and skills, but who does not recover from the setback, and continues to struggle just to make ends meet.

We will learn about a single father, who lost his wife to the coronavirus only days after he was let go from his consulting firm due to a COVID-19 "restructuring," who learns to code and eventually creates a thriving tech company. Similarly, we will read about someone who faced the same tragedy but fell into a deep depression and remained there for a decade.

Stories like these highlight something that is much more powerful than even resilience, which is loosely defined as facing something challenging and bouncing back to the same place you were. An extremely important skill to be sure, but these types of outcomes highlight Nicholas Nassim Taleb's, "antifragililty," a concept he developed that holds that some things actually thrive and grow as a result of shocks, volatility, stress, failure, setbacks, and so on.[1] How is it that multiple people can be struck by astonishingly similar catastrophes and some wither while others thrive? If the situation is the same, where does the difference lay? The difference is in the reaction or response of the person facing the situation.

I hope it's clear to you by now that mindfulness isn't going to magically change your life by preventing bad things from ever happening to you. It can, however, change your life by giving you access to choice, which automatic reaction robs of you. Changing your response to life is often as good as changing your life.

Responding versus Reacting

Would you rather work for a reactive leader who goes on a tirade when the client you pitched last week awards the work to another firm or a responsive leader who pulls together the team to analyze how to do better next time? Would you rather date a person who reacts automatically when the restaurant messes up the order or who responds thoughtfully to address the situation? Would you rather go on a dangerous intelligence collection mission into a war zone with someone who reacts blindly to incoming enemy fire or someone who responds rapidly with deliberate action and precision?

Intuitively, we know responding thoughtfully to challenging situations and people is more likely to lead to optimal outcomes. However, we often fall into reactive patterns triggered by even the smallest things, such as when someone criticizes our work or disagrees with us in a meeting. The husband who snaps at his wife for merely asking him if he put away the laundry yet knows all too well the painful realization that responding thoughtfully would have been a wiser course of action than reacting automatically. This is the difference between merely an intellectual understanding that responding is wiser and true embodied wisdom.

Let's look at the qualities of a reaction and a response.[2] This also may be intuitive, but I believe it's helpful to highlight these concepts in more concrete terms so that they are easier to identify in our lives.

Reactions come immediately and automatically without deliberate thought. They are driven by our previous experiences, beliefs, habits, biases, as well as from the brain's survival center, the limbic system, where that fight-or-flight reaction we talked about in Chapter 12 comes from. The fight-or-flight system comes online when you feel threatened, fearful, or challenged, which is a good thing if it's reacting to a tiger but not so good when it's your wife asking you about the laundry. That said, reactions are not always "wrong." For example, the automatic reaction of pulling your hand away when inadvertently touching a hot pan is a helpful automatic reaction.

Responses are conscious choices and often come more slowly due to the thoughtful consideration that is taking place in the brain. You can never fully escape some influence from the unconscious mind, so that will still be there, but responses will include consideration of the first-, second-, and third-order implications of your actions, also known as consequences. Responses aren't always the "right" or "best" thing to do, but they are choices, they produce less needless suffering, and you have a better chance at taking deliberate action that is aligned with your values and goals.

There is so little we control in our lives. We didn't decide which era we would be born into or which country. We had no say in who our biological parents would be nor their economic situation. We didn't select our babysitters or our elementary, middle, or high school teachers. We don't control whether the car coming in the opposite direction will suddenly swerve into our lane. The ability to respond to whatever life throws at you is one of the most powerful skills a human can cultivate.

Victor Frankl, the Austrian psychiatrist who survived the holocaust, says in his book *Man's Search for Meaning*, "Between stimulus and response there is a space. In that space is our power to choose our response. In our response lies our growth and our freedom." Are you automatically reacting to life or responding to it? Our daily decisions in this space determine the direction and quality of our lives. Take a look at Table 13.1 for some examples of difficult life situations (stimulus) and how our brain might automatically react to protect our ego or with harshness toward oneself, contrasted with accepting the situation (it's already here) and responding in a more thoughtful and empowering way.

Can you see how the harsh self-attack or ego-protecting reactive mind might lead to compounding problems such as lower self-confidence, anxiety, depression, and general unhappiness? Conversely, can you see how a thoughtful response that takes a wider perspective has a greater likelihood to lead to a more empowering position from which to process and manage the setback? Notice, too, I am not saying we have to *like* the setback, failure, or tragedy. It's perfectly natural to not like being sick or having our parents pass away, but when our automatic reactive story makes it seem like the universe has it out to get us personally, it adds a layer of optional misery. Life is challenging enough on its own without our creating a miserable and disempowering story to go along with it. You are the author of your life; pick up the pen and write a better story. Furthermore, not everything that is uncomfortable or painful is bad for you.

So, how do you move the needle from habitual reactivity to thoughtful response? Consistent and diligent training. In my career as

TABLE **13.1** Responding thoughtfully to the inevitable challenges in life reduces needless suffering.

Challenging Life Situations	Reactions That Lead to Suffering	Responses That Prevent Suffering
Inevitable	Automatic (but optional with training)	Deliberate choice (with training)
Pain	Resistance: this shouldn't be happening to me.	Acceptance (not necessarily liking): What's the message?
Failure	Self-attack: I'm an idiot; someone else's fault; non-acceptance.	Healthy self-view: What can I learn? I can improve.
Lost job	Someone else's fault; attack others or self; non-acceptance.	This sucks but I can recover; there is opportunity here.
Passed over for promotion	Victim mentality; attack others or self; non-acceptance.	Healthy self-view: What can I learn?; I can improve.
Someone disagrees with you	Attack mode; I'm right, you're wrong; non-acceptance.	People have different opinions and that's okay.
Someone doesn't like you	Self-attack; what's wrong with me?; attack others; non-acceptance.	People like people who fit their paradigm for friend. I don't fit their paradigm and that's okay.
Illness	This shouldn't be happening to me; non-acceptance.	Getting sick is normal, even if I eat right, exercise, and get enough sleep.
Loved one dies	Why me; non-acceptance.	Why not me? Of course, people in my life will die. It's also absolutely okay to be sad about it.

a soldier and intelligence officer, I was required to undergo various intense and realistic training scenarios, such as crossing a border in alias, driving vehicles at high speeds through road blocks, being kidnapped from a public street, hooded, berated, and interrogated, picking handcuffs while blindfolded in the trunk of a car, being attacked by men with batons, and much more. The few men and women in the military and intelligence community who go through this type of specialized training, do so to learn to keep their wits about them and make solid decisions under the most dangerous and high-pressure situations you can imagine. This training does not feel good on any

level, except when it's over, and it's never over as long as you remain
in the job. Dedicating one's life or even a portion of one's life to that
type of work is to commit to turning toward and accepting the very
uncomfortable emotions, sensations, and experiences that tend to
accompany an operational career. It's that act of consistently turning
toward and fully facing difficulty that cultivates the ability to respond
deliberately and thoughtfully, despite the human tendency to react
automatically out of fear, anger, stress, or resentment. It doesn't mean
fear, stress, or other challenging emotions are absent; it means they
aren't driving the action.

Our main practice this week, Delving into the Difficult, is designed
to help you, at your own pace, turn toward a difficult situation in
your life and see if you can sit with any uncomfortable sensations,
emotions, and reactive thoughts that arise and just notice them, letting go of any effort to push or wish them away.

Think of it like this: uncomfortable experiences, sensations, and
emotions are just as much a part of this life as pleasurable ones and,
like your overly political relative, they are coming to the reunion
whether you want them to or not, so you might as well get used
to having them visit from time to time without picking a fight and
making everything worse for everyone.

■ ■ ■

As I mentioned, I would be clear when I ask you to do a meditation that is not mindfulness. This next meditation, Delving into the
Difficult, is one such meditation. Although there is a component
of mindfulness within the meditation, it's not strictly mindfulness
because we will be deliberately bringing difficult thoughts or experiences into our meditation instead of merely noticing what comes
up on its own.

You can read through the following meditation transcript and
then do the exercise on your own without any guidance. However,
especially if you are new to this, I recommend doing it as a guided
meditation by listening to the audio files noted in the Resources, my
teacher account on the Insight Timer app, or at http://www.clifsmith
.com; see Appendix page 189 for details. The audio guidance will
help you stay on track until you are comfortable and/or interested in
doing the exercise on your own.

Delving into the Difficult Meditation

In this meditation[3] we will be deliberately bringing up difficult situations; therefore, please use your best judgment regarding what you choose to "work" with during the exercise. It's best not to start with the most traumatic situation in your life. We are delving into the difficult, not diving into it. Once you get the hang of being able to sit with discomfort, I do recommend gradually moving to the edge of your comfort zone where real growth can occur. If at any time during this meditation things become overwhelming, you can discontinue the exercise. Let's begin.

- ◆ Begin by taking a seated posture and settle in for the exercise. Once you're reasonably settled, allow the eyes to close, and tune into your attention and awareness, just noticing whatever is here in the mind and body for a few moments. Allow whatever you notice to be just as it is and let go of any impulse to wish things to be different or wish them away.
- ◆ Bring your awareness to the breath as we have been practicing. Notice the sensations of breathing where you feel them most prominently. Become aware of the full duration of each inbreath and each outbreath.
- ◆ Anticipation of working with a difficultly or other thoughts may be arising; this is fine. Let's use this opportunity now to try out this new exercise. Previously, if we had gotten captivated by a thought or a story, we would have caught it, acknowledged it, and brought our attention back to the breath. The call, in this exercise, is to notice the thoughts, stories, and emotions carrying the difficulty, allowing them to remain on the main stage of our awareness, turning toward them to see them clearly. Then delve into where the difficulty may be showing up in the body by noticing any physical sensations that the difficulty may have brought with it. The sensations may be very subtle or readily noticed, but in either case see if you can recognize sensations that accompany the particular difficulty you're working with. When you

recognize the sensations associated with the difficulty, focus your attention on them just as you would in the body scan, with a curious and nonjudgmental approach.

♦ If no difficulties have arisen, I invite you to bring to mind a difficulty currently affecting your life. Remember there's no need to start with the most difficult or traumatic situation but instead something you are open to exploring and that brings up feelings of unpleasantness, annoyance, regret, or even anger. Something current is most useful, but if nothing arises from your present circumstances, you can bring up something from the past to work with.

♦ Bring this situation to mind and see it as vividly as you can on the main stage of your awareness. Then delve into where the difficulty is showing up in the body and bring the spotlight of attention to explore the sensations you find here.

♦ Use the spotlight of attention to delve into the sensations more deeply, noticing their quality. Notice whether they are static, changing, increasing, or decreasing in intensity. Notice, as well, any automatic reactions that may be coming up. Meet whatever is coming up with acceptance, patience, and nonjudgmental curiosity, allowing it all to be on the main stage of awareness.

♦ If pushing away or other impulses to change or eliminate the sensations arise, there's no need to criticize yourself. Acknowledge that not wanting difficult experiences or sensations is natural but see if it's possible to allow them to remain on the main stage of awareness for a while.

♦ Continue to shine the spotlight of attention on these sensations. Catch and Release any resistance to being open to these unpleasant sensations and experiences in this moment. Acknowledge that resistance to unpleasant things is an automatic reaction but see if there's space to be open to them and still be okay.

♦ You may find that the sensations fade after a while. Then you can decide whether to bring the difficult situation to mind again or a new one, as vividly as you can and again

continued

delving into the area of the body where the difficulty is showing up.

♦ Bring attention now back to noticing the sensations of breathing. Pay clear focused attention to where you feel the body breathing most prominently. Notice the full duration of each inbreath and each outbreath.

♦ As the exercise comes to a close, acknowledge whatever courage and strength it required to turn toward and delve into this difficulty today. Know that building this skill leads to a greater ability to navigate life's ups and downs with a bit more ease.

♦ I invite you to open your eyes if you've closed them and bring your attention back into the room you're in. Give yourself a moment to get your bearings before moving into the next part of your day.

Common Themes, Challenges, and Questions

Are you saying I have to accept a bad situation such as being in an unhealthy relationship or accepting a demeaning and aggressive boss? Not at all. Practicing accepting and opening to uncomfortable emotions, sensations, and experiences is not about learning to resign oneself to a *changeable* situation. Acceptance in this context could be described as willingness to see reality in this moment as it is, as opposed to denying reality and turning away from it automatically because of some internal discomfort, fear, anxiety, stress, or ego protection. Once you can accept reality for what it is and are seeing it more clearly, you can apply mindfulness to it and respond deliberately versus reacting automatically. Seeing a situation more clearly can also help you determine if it is even changeable or if it's your perspective/reactivity that might be a part of the overall challenge and perhaps a change within you is in order.

Won't I be bullied or be a pushover if I just accept everything? Again, this is not about giving up or giving in to harsh or unfair treatment. This is about accepting a situation as it is in the moment and responding instead of automatically reacting. Let's take a sports example. I presume you've heard of the phrase "talking trash." One situation in which this often occurs is on the basketball court when a player is about to take a free throw shot. Players on the opposing team often hurl insults or comments designed to put the shooter off balance or make him angry so they miss the shot. Falling into reactive mode and getting angry is the worst thing that can happen for the shooter. Wouldn't it be better to accept that "trash talking" is a part of the game and not fall into self-protective reaction but instead respond deliberately by continuing to focus on the task at hand? Sometimes not responding is the best response! Being the recipient of someone talking trash is out of your control. Are you going to give that person power over you by automatically reacting every time that person hurls an insult or criticism your way; who is in charge if that's the case? In my experience, not being bothered by a bully's idiotic comments is much more likely to annoy that person.

What do you mean when you say just because something is uncomfortable doesn't mean it's bad for you? There are a couple levels here we can delve into. A legitimately challenging workout is likely to bring some discomfort with it, but it is usually good for our health to go through that discomfort. Setbacks that are uncomfortable to endure are often doors of opportunity to greater things we could have never imagined. Losing a job spurs you to finally start that business. Going through the heartbreaking stages of a relationship ending when you wanted, with all your being, for it to continue, but then you meet and end up with someone who makes you grateful that the previous relationship failed. We can realize in the midst of setbacks, challenges, and heartbreaks that they are part of the process of life and often clear the way for the next chapter. And then there are the very minor things we amplify and darken our own moods with. We often recoil from challenging, annoying, or uncomfortable things that, if we paid closer attention, have within them the seeds of something we can actually put on a list of things we could be grateful for having. Let's go through some examples. I don't like to do my taxes. It's complicated, annoying, and there's always some rule change I have to deal with before filing. Woe is me, right? At least I have a job. The "discomfort" of having to do taxes might be someone else's dream; people construct rafts out of PVC pipe and shoestrings and put their lives in danger crossing parts of the ocean for the privilege of doing their taxes someday. Here's another one. I hate cleaning the toilet in my house; it's so gross. Seriously, it's like my 5-year-old son deliberately aims everywhere but the "bullseye." After a party, forget about it; it's absolutely disgusting. Those complaints are automatic reactions and they themselves make cleaning the toilet more "difficult" than it actually is and, on top of that, the mind doesn't automatically bring up the fact that it's pretty nice to have a house in the first place. This automatic omission is a habitual reaction, too. We see what's "wrong" with a situation, what's inconvenient, what "puts us out," and we give nary a thought to the, dare I say, blessings of such "challenges." This is not to say you have to like these setbacks and challenging situations, but why would anyone want to stay stuck in a demotivating and mood-killing internal narrative that just makes it all worse, especially when it's optional. As we say in the military, "embrace the suck"; complaining about it only makes it worse for you and everyone in earshot.

What if I'm not ready to face some challenging emotions? That's perfectly fine. You are your best advocate here, and this process will help you discover your own boundaries. If you want to hold off doing this exercise, you can continue with previous meditations until you are ready. Also, you get to choose which difficult situations to work with during the exercises, so you can dip your toe into the difficult before diving into it. It's best not to start with the most difficult, emotionally charged, or traumatic situation in any case. The call here is to find the edges of your comfort zone and push into them slightly if that's where you are and bring some self-compassion to the table, perhaps in the form of a self-directed comment: "It's perfectly fine not to like this; let's just see if I can sit with it for a few moments, and if not, that's okay, too." This is the work of a lifetime, not a long weekend. There is no need to rush.

Key Points, Practices, and Signposts

Key Points
- Responses are deliberate choices and may come more slowly (although this changes with training). Responding to life is often just as powerful as changing one's life circumstances.
- Reactions are automatic and they come from our past experiences, beliefs, habits, biases, and the brain's survival center. When we react, we are imprisoned by our past and are often making an already difficult situation more challenging.

◆ We can learn to respond more wisely to difficult situations by training ourselves to turn toward them and recognize we can be uncomfortable and still be okay. Not everything that is uncomfortable is bad for you. As we learn to keep our wits about us, even during difficult situations, we'll be better equipped to respond while taking in a wider perspective, leading to more optimal results.

Formal Practices
◆ Awareness of Breath meditation—twice a day for at least 10 to 15 minutes per session. (Chapter 6, page 58 or http://www.clifsmith.com)
◆ Delving into the Difficult meditation—once a day for 7 days. (Chapter 13, page 136 or http://www.clifsmith.com)

Informal Practices
◆ Mindful walking—every day. (Appendix page 192)
◆ Catch and Release—Catch and Release one unhelpful internal belief, judgment, or thought each day. (Appendix page 191)
◆ S.T.O.P. practice—as needed. (Appendix page 192)
◆ Gratitude journal—before bed, write down one to three things you are grateful for from the day. What you are grateful for can be big or small.

Signposts
◆ As you consistently practice the Delving into the Difficult meditation, you may notice less reactivity to external setbacks as well as to self-generated fearful, anxious, or stress-filled thoughts. But this will take time, and having less reactivity in one instance doesn't mean you won't be reactive the next time, especially if you cease practicing. It's just like working out; muscles atrophy when not exercised.
◆ You might begin to notice that many of the reactive thoughts in response to difficult situations are just attempts at keeping us safe from perceived threats we picked up when we were younger. Following them now may not be

continued

wise, and it can be profoundly liberating to notice how much we may have been standing in our own way.

♦ As you begin to respond to situations and difficult interactions in which you previously reacted, you may see that the experience of the interaction improves despite no or little change in the circumstances. When this happens, you may get a glimpse of a path to happiness and contentment that cannot be taken from you.

Chapter 14

Week 6: In the Same Boat

Some of the most meaningful and most challenging moments in our lives involve our relationships with others. If you've ever had a significant other you probably know, all too well, both those types of moments often come in the same relationship! It's not just relationships with our significant other that this occurs; our professional and other personal relationships also have this type of experience. It's time now to pivot to the practical. I shared previously that you don't work out in the gym to be fit in the gym; you work out in the gym so you are fit and healthy for life outside the gym. Let's take our mindfulness skills out of the gym and into our interactions with others, as we drop in on another situation between Alice and Sarah from Chapter 11. Alice is still up for partner and although she is working in the same group as Sarah, she no longer reports directly to her.[1]

On Friday afternoon about 4:40 pm, Alice received an email from Sarah:

Hi Alice!

I hope you are doing well. I'm in a bit of a bind. Remember that work you helped us win last month with Reggie's company? The engagement just started last week and Reggie has asked for the digital transformation plan we pitched to be updated with a new time line; he wants everything delayed by 6 months. Because you were part of the original proposal team that won the work, you have all the data and documentation needed to make the updates as well as an understanding of the details. The new team isn't as familiar with the project yet. Could you help me out by updating those documents and note the impact of the shift?

My meeting with Reggie is first thing Monday, so I really need the documents back by tomorrow afternoon, or Sunday evening at the latest, to give me time to review them before the meeting. Let me know either way and if you can do it, please feel free to reach out anytime if you have any questions. This is important.

Thanks,
Sarah

Alice has plans for the weekend but this is an important client and Sarah has been supportive so she decides to cancel her plans and update the documents. The updates were a bit more complicated than she expected so she sends them to Sarah on Sunday morning.

On Monday morning when Alice opens her email, she sees the following note from Sarah in her inbox:

I'm about to walk into my meeting with Reggie and it is not going to go well. I just looked at the documents and the milestone dates in the time line are all wrong! How could you let this happen? I need you to update the files again but this time with the correct dates. The first milestone should be February 1 not December 1, so you didn't capture the impact on their financials due to the first phase of the transformation crossing the calendar year. Let's talk ASAP after I'm out of this meeting at 9 am. I'll need the updates back by the end of the day.

Sarah
Sent from mobile

Alice stands up, goes and gets herself a cup of coffee, puts creamer in it, stirs slowly, and walks back to her desk to make the call at 9:15 am.

"Hi Sarah, it's Alice."

"Oh, thank God, what took you so long? Never mind. I need those files back as soon as possible, no later than the end of the day. I was so embarrassed at that meeting. How could you get those dates wrong? I told you this was important."

"What are you talking about, Sarah? I updated the files just like you asked. You said 'everything is delayed by 6 months,' so I went through all the documents across the entire 5-year plan and updated each milestone and decision gate with the new data and impact of the shifted time line."

"It looks like you shifted the time line from June 1 to December 1; that's not correct—"

Alice interrupts, "Yes, it is. That's 6 months from first milestone in the proposal I pitched. I have it right here in front of me."

"It's *not* correct! We moved that initial date to August 1 on the first day of the engagement; they even talked about the possibility of that move during your pitch. So, the shift should have been from August 1 to February 1."

"How was I supposed to know they *actually* changed the date instead of just thinking about it? I assumed 6 months from the proposal."

"You could have picked up the phone to ask or confirm."

"You asked me to do the update because I had the documents from the proposal and said I had all the information I needed! And, didn't you say you wanted the documents this weekend so you could review. I don't seem to have a note from you on Sunday with this important bit of information."

"I have a lot of things going on and thought I could trust you. Are you going to fix it or not?"

"Fine. Yes, I'll update them, but I have other deadlines today, too."

"This must be done by the end of the day."

■ ■ ■

In my previous profession, E&E stood for escape and evasion. The goal was to avoid the enemy at all costs so one could get back to a safe and secure location in "friendly" territory. In the often messy and complicated interactions with other humans, we sometimes view them as enemies threatening our safety and security, so we automatically react in ways that protect our egos, reputations, and identities and avoid seeing the situation from the other person's point of view or seeking to understand. Therefore, I offer a new meaning and purpose of E&E—Empathize And Engage—with the overall goal of understanding, so we can better connect, collaborate, and cohabitate.

In the conversation between Alice and Sarah, there is no empathy nor attempts to understand, but, instead, there is a great deal of automatic reaction focused on assigning blame. They each seem to be under the impression that if the blame rests with the other person, then they themselves haven't contributed to the problem. This is a recipe for continued friction and, even when the files are updated and the client is satisfied, the relationship between Alice and Sarah will likely continue to be tension filled.

What would you do in this situation? Who is right? Sarah thinks Alice is to blame because she didn't pick up the phone to verify her assumptions. Alice thinks Sarah is to blame because she didn't give her all the information she needed and didn't review the work in time to make changes before the meeting like she said she would. The fact that the time line is not accurate and did not get delivered to the client is not in dispute; the conversation here is about blame, and it is occurring through the lens of interpretation and judgment.

Let's take it another layer deeper to see what might be going on within Alice and Sarah as this entire conversation was unfolding. See Table 14.1.

These thoughts, interpretations, and judgments are going to create and/or intensify each of their emotional reactions, which will further affect their thinking. Plus, there's a lot going on beyond the overt conversation. Alice may be feeling unappreciated, angry, annoyed, confused, regretful, fearful, and feeling like she was set up to fail. Sarah might be experiencing regret, anger, confusion, annoyance, and fear, as well.

You may be asking, why is fear on the list of things they might be feeling in this situation? First, notice that neither of them are taking responsibility for any contribution to the mistake. No one wants

TABLE **14.1** What Alice and Sarah are thinking during the conversation.

Alice	Sarah
I cancelled my weekend plans to help her out when I didn't have to and she doesn't even appreciate it.	Why did I even trust her with this? What a mistake.
She should have told me about the initial date change and could have reviewed the document earlier like she said she would.	The fact that she didn't even reach out to the team to verify the dates is a bad sign.
I have better things to do than help her with her work. I'll get this fixed for her and then never again!	Maybe it's not such a good decision to promote her.

to be blamed. Sarah certainly isn't accepting any blame and may be feeling some fear that going out on a limb and supporting Alice's promotion has been a mistake or that her rapport with the client has taken a hit.

Alice, however, is likely feeling some fear and anxiety that this will affect her partner promotion. Also, if she is feeling set up, she is assigning intent to Sarah's actions, that is, "Sarah did this on purpose to sabotage me," which would certainly create some fear.

This brings us to intent in general. We often automatically assume intent based on the emotion we feel in reaction to a comment or situation. For example, if my wife says, "Are you going to work out today?" I might feel put down and automatically assume she intended to insult me and make me feel bad, when, in reality, maybe she was just asking so she could coordinate our schedules. This automatic application of intent to others' actions has ruined many a friendship and relationship because it doesn't only affect your emotional reaction, it also creates stories in your head about the other person's character. Believing your wife deliberately put you down might lead to thoughts such as, "How could my wife be so deliberately mean to me. What kind of callous person does that?" It can be difficult to have fruitful interactions with anyone you've already decided lacks morals or has a malevolent character. I encourage you to apply Catch and Release as much to the automatic process of assuming intent as you do other unhelpful beliefs, judgments, and thoughts.

Finally, there is an even deeper layer of fear of what being responsible for this mistake might say about them personally, as competent consultants, leaders, or individuals.

We tend to go through great lengths, unconsciously, to protect our self-image, and it can wreak havoc on our ability to recognize our role in difficult situations and relationships. Furthermore, this incessant need to keep our self-image intact can keep us from moving on or growing into new phases of our lives, such as a CEO whose business fails and is so wrapped up in his identity as a CEO or leader that he won't take a "step down" into a non-CEO job. Not only is he still not a CEO, he fails to realize that you have to pull a slingshot back to launch the stone forward. Stepping "back" or "down" isn't always capitulation. Similarly, being willing to acknowledge your role in some mistake or misunderstanding is not a sign of weakness or incompetence. On the contrary, that kind of vulnerability (willingness to acknowledge your role or fault) is a sign of self-confidence. It's the person who can never admit his or her culpability who is insecure and must protect a very fragile ego.

The reality is that there are very few disagreements or arguments that are totally caused by one person alone, so to work through them successfully, you must learn to Catch and Release the automatic reactivity and take deliberate steps to Empathize and Engage in order to understand the other person's perspective.

■ ■ ■

There are two new practices you'll do this week to grow your ability to Empathize and Engage to understand others in your interactions. The first is called the S.P.A.R.R. practice, which stands for Stop, Pause, Assess, Recognize, and Respond.[2] S.P.A.R.R. gives us a moment to step out of habitual reactivity and into deliberate choice when a comment comes our way that leads to being "triggered" or having other unhelpful automatic reactions likely to exacerbate the interaction if we act on them blindly. You can use S.P.A.R.R. when it begins to feel like someone is *sparring* with you, so you can keep your cool during the exchange. You're sparring too but not in the same way. We'll explain S.P.A.R.R. in a bit more detail below and apply it to Alice and Sarah's situation shortly.

The second practice will be a non-mindfulness meditation called In the Same Boat, which is designed to remind ourselves how similar we are to other people, to highlight that we share common experiences, and to show us that we are essentially "in the same boat" going through this life. This meditation increases our ability to empathize, encourages understanding and connection, and lays the foundation for compassion, which we'll discuss in the next chapter.

S.P.A.R.R.ing during Difficult Interactions

Let's look at the S.P.A.R.R. practice more closely and see how applying it to the Alice and Sarah situation might have affected the interaction and relationship differently than the reactive modes that played out earlier. The following defines each step of S.P.A.R.R. more clearly.

S—Stop as soon as you catch that a comment has triggered an automatic reaction within you or **Stop** in response to a comment or question in another context that may be important to you to respond thoughtfully.

P—Pause for a moment to gather yourself and complete the next steps.

A—Assess what emotions and thoughts you are aware of in yourself and that may be in the person you're talking to during the interaction and assess what a wiser course of action might be, as opposed to going with your automatic reaction. You may want to confirm the other person's emotions and thoughts during the Respond step if appropriate, because, as we've seen, our interpretations can be wildly inaccurate. Part of inquiring about thoughts and emotions without judgment is to acknowledge them in the other person. This requires that you pay attention and listen during the interaction.

R—Recognize there is a human being on the other end of the communication and acknowledge, accept, and be open to that person's situation, agenda, and point of view. This doesn't mean you have to agree with the person; it's more about trying to understand and exercising empathy. If you keep your own agenda as the primary motivation for the interaction, you will miss out on information the person is sending, and you won't build trust because that person will know that you are more interested in what you want than you are in understanding them.

R—Respond deliberately and in a way that supports effective communication.

S.P.A.R.R. requires giving your full attention to the interaction in the present moment, which you should be doing anyway 6 weeks into this program. S.P.A.R.R. can then be used in the midst of the conversation to become more aware of your and the other person's inner weather pattern, the thoughts and feelings that might be influencing your and their behaviors. It creates the time to turn toward and be open to what the other person may be experiencing, what that person's agenda is, and it can be done without you having to agree. As you deliberately engage in this process, you are helping improve your odds of moving from automatic reaction to a more thoughtful and wise response to the situation. Instead of just waiting for your turn to talk and push your agenda, you'll be listening to understand and that builds trust.

What if Alice had used S.P.A.R.R on her call with Sarah? Let's take a look:

"Hi Sarah, it's Alice."

"Oh, thank God, what took you so long? Never mind. I need those files back as soon as possible, no later than the end of the day. I was so embarrassed at that meeting. How could you get those dates wrong? I told you this was important."

"What are you talking about, Sarah? I updated the files just like you asked. You said 'everything is delayed by 6 months,' so I went through all the documents across the entire 5-year plan and updated each milestone and decision gate with the new data and impact of the shifted time line." (We may not catch our emotions rising right away and that's okay. We can apply S.P.A.R.R. as soon as we notice automatic reactivity. Plus, this seems like a reasonable response.)

"It looks like you shifted the time line from June 1 to December 1; that's not correct. . . We moved that initial date to August 1 on the first day of the engagement. . . So, the shift should have been from August 1 to February 1."

Alice invokes S.P.A.R.R.

S—Stop (Feeling attacked and reactive; about to cut Sarah off but stopping to let her finish)
P—Pause (. . .)
A—Assess (It sounds like Sarah is really upset right now and me yelling back or cutting her off probably won't help.)
R—Recognize (Sarah is under a lot of pressure, too.)
R—Respond (I don't want to escalate the situation. I'll acknowledge what she might be feeling and share the details from my perspective.)

"Sarah, I can tell you're upset and I imagine it was not pleasant going into that meeting with Reggie without the accurate information. I had no idea the time line changed. I was using the proposal documentation from the day we pitched. I guess I could have called you to double-check, but that's why I thought you asked me to help in the first place, so we could leverage the documents from the pitch and turn this around quickly. Believe me, I would rather have not canceled my beach plans but could tell this was important to you and the firm."

"Yes, that *is* why I reached out to you. I realize now I forgot to mention the date change. Then Sunday rolled around and my son got sick so I wasn't able to even look at the documents until right before the meeting."

Alice invokes S.P.A.R.R.

S—Stop (Less agitated and still keen to respond thoughtfully.)

P—Pause (. . .)

A—Assess (A high pressure deadline, a sick kid, and now an unhappy client—how might I be able to help?)

R—Recognize (Just two of those things would be stressful for anyone—her reaction is understandable; even if it's misdirected at me, it's probably not intentional.)

R—Respond (Ask about her son and focus on solutions instead of blame.)

"How's your son?"

"He's okay but was throwing up all night."

"That's no fun; I hope he feels better. How did Reggie react and who from your team can I work with to get these documents updated again? I have a deadline today on my new project that I still have to meet but want to make sure we handle this together."

"Thanks, Alice. You know Reggie; he's pretty laid back, but I was so frazzled because of my son, being tired, and just realizing right before walking in that the document wasn't what he wanted. Sorry I was short with you in my email and when we started this call. I think Kiran is available to help, too. I really appreciate you helping me out on this.

"No worries. I'm happy to help. Get some sleep tonight if you can!"

The power of S.P.A.R.R. in this scenario, is that it not only prevented escalation but also it enabled Alice and Sarah to acknowledge that they both played a role in the situation. Alice's approach of addressing how Sarah might be feeling was a smart move because feelings and emotions, despite the corporate world often ignoring them, are a part of all contentious conversations. It displayed empathy and signaled to Sarah that Alice was listening to understand, not just listening (or cutting her off) to respond with her "side of the story." Notice, too, that responding with empathy and engaging thoughtfully to understand did not prevent Alice from sharing her perspective. In fact, it enabled her perspective to be more effectively heard by Sarah.

Of course, not all S.P.A.R.R.ing will go like this; I do have to make it look good in the book. The idea is that by catching your reactivity and invoking this technique, you are *more likely* to avoid the common pitfalls associated with reacting automatically to the brain's perceived threats that occur in a contentious or emotionally charged conversation. And, even if it doesn't go as well as you would have liked, if you've kept your wits about you and responded versus reacted, you can walk away knowing you didn't contribute to making matters worse.

S.P.A.R.R. can be brought to bear on a number of interactions in person, in emails, via text messages, and on the phone to help you be much more thoughtful and deliberate in your responses. It's helpful when being interviewed for a job, responding to client objections or concerns during a pitch, discussing rules with your teenager, talking with your spouse or partner, dealing with authorities, and even responding to an email in which someone has thrown you under the bus. Any time you are having a conversation that might have some increased emotional energy tied to it, S.P.A.R.R. can help you navigate that interaction more wisely.

▪ ▪ ▪

Although S.P.A.R.R. is a useful tool, it does not, on its own, increase your ability to empathize and put yourself in another person's shoes. That's where the In the Same Boat meditation comes in to help us flex and strengthen our empathy muscles. We'll talk more about empathy in Chapter 15, but this meditation is the first step in cultivating this important ability. Additionally, similar to Delving into the Difficult, the In the Same Boat meditation is not a mindfulness meditation because we will be deliberately invoking certain aspects of our life and experiences to strengthen, in this case, empathy.

You can read through the following meditation transcript and then do the exercise on your own without any guidance. However, especially if you are new to this, I recommend doing it as a guided meditation by listening to the audio files noted in the Resources, my teacher account on the Insight Timer app, or at http://www.clifsmith. com; see Appendix page 189 for details. The audio guidance will help you stay on track until you are comfortable and/or interested in doing the exercise on your own.

In the Same Boat Meditation

In this empathy-building meditation,[3] we will be reminding ourselves how similar other people are to us and that we are "in the same boat" of life, facing similar challenges, meeting with the same inevitable ups and downs, and navigating life as best we can. Acknowledging these similarities helps create the mental habit of perceiving common humanity with others, as well as lay the foundation for further compassion- and kindness-building exercises. This exercise can help inform how we interact with others, allowing us to Empathize and Engage, even when we are in a disagreement with someone.

Let's begin.

◆ Begin by taking a seated posture and settling in for the exercise. Once you're reasonably settled, allow the eyes to close if that's comfortable; otherwise, lower your gaze and soften your focus and tune into your attention and awareness, just noticing whatever is here in the mind and body for a few moments. Allow whatever you notice to be just as it is and let go of any impulse to wish things to be different or wish them away.

◆ Hold the body with an attitude of unconditional friendliness and care.

◆ Begin to sense the movement of the breath in the heart area, near the center of the chest.

◆ Allow yourself to bring to mind someone with whom you have a positive and uncomplicated relationship. It can be anyone: a child, friend, family member, neighbor, or colleague.

◆ As they appear on the main stage of awareness, silently repeat the following phrases to yourself:

◆ We are in the same boat of life.
◆ We both have a body and a mind.
◆ We both have thoughts and emotions.
◆ We both have been sad, disappointed, angry, hurt, or confused.
◆ We have both experienced physical and emotional pain and suffering.

continued

- ◆ We both wish to be free of pain and suffering.
- ◆ We have both experienced happiness and joy.
- ◆ We both wish to be healthy, happy, and loved.

- ◆ Let go of this person and now bring to mind someone with whom you may not get along so well. Perhaps it's someone you have friction with from time to time; it's best not to start with the most challenging person but someone who it's not as easy to wish well.
- ◆ As that person appears on the main stage of awareness, silently repeat the following phrases to yourself:

  - ◆ We are in the same boat of life.
  - ◆ We both have a body and a mind.
  - ◆ We both have thoughts and emotions.
  - ◆ We both have been sad, disappointed, angry, hurt, or confused.
  - ◆ We have both experienced physical and emotional pain and suffering.
  - ◆ We both wish to be free of pain and suffering.
  - ◆ We have both experienced happiness and joy.
  - ◆ We both wish to be healthy, happy, and loved.

- ◆ Notice whatever sensations and feelings arise and sit with them for a few moments. Let go of any impulse to wish things to be different or wish them away.
- ◆ Now return attention to the breath for the last few moments of this exercise. Notice the full duration of each inbreath and outbreath.
- ◆ I invite you to open your eyes if you've closed them and bring attention back into the room you're in. Give yourself a moment to get your bearings before moving into the next part of your day.

Common Themes, Challenges, and Questions
What if a disagreement or fight is all someone else's fault? Why should I go through all this to thoughtfully respond when that person is the one to blame? It's almost certainly not true that

a disagreement is all someone else's fault. If there are two people in the disagreement, there are at least two people contributing to it in some way. Contribution does not equal blame; it means you've contributed in some way to the tenor and outcome of the interaction. If you focus on blame, you miss out on the opportunity to learn the other person's perspective, interpretations, and judgments, which can lead to understanding (not necessarily agreeing). There is another reason, too, to continue to cultivate thoughtful responses over automatic reactivity. Who is in control if you automatically react every time someone does something you don't agree with or that is annoying to you? Automatically reacting gives your power away, and being able to respond in any given situation is a superpower.

S.P.A.R.R. seems like it would take an awfully long time to use in the moment. Wouldn't it slow down every conversation? Just about anything you do the first time may feel cumbersome for a while. Plus, we are often so wrapped up in our own agenda, it will take practice to deliberately release that tendency for a moment so we can actually listen to the person across from us. The more you go through the process, the more quickly you'll be flowing through steps as a natural part of how you interact with others. It's kind of like the S.T.O.P. practice in that regard. At this point in time, if you've been doing the S.T.O.P. practice the last 5 or 6 weeks it's probably coming more naturally to you. This will happen with S.P.A.R.R., too. The more you use it, the more you'll be able to do so in the future, particularly when you must navigate challenging and contentious conversations.

I actually got quite emotional and cried when I did the In the Same Boat meditation. Is that normal? When we do an exercise in which we are bringing to mind others who we have some emotional connection to (pleasant or unpleasant) and deliberately express empathy or compassion for them, it has the potential to "stir the pot" a bit. That is to say, it can bring up unresolved situations or unprocessed emotions that might lead to more intense emotions during the practice. Exploring the edges of your comfort zone with curiosity and compassion or stopping the practice altogether is something you'll have to decide, as is the decision to reach out for professional psychological guidance if you feel it's needed. If you find that the emotions are overwhelming and/or consistently tied to a specific person, that may be a sign that talking to a professional might be beneficial. There is no weakness in asking for help; quite the contrary.

Key Points, Practices, and Signposts

Key Points

- Instead of reacting automatically to protect our self-image or ego during a disagreement or contentious conversation, deliberately Empathize and Engage with the goal of understanding. Understanding does not mean agreeing; it's a willingness to hear the other person's perspective, story, interpretation, and so on.
- Remember to S.P.A.R.R. when conversations get contentious or you're feeling attacked. Your ability to remain steady and keep your wits about you despite the intensity of the interaction will pay dividends in the long run.
- We are more alike than we are different. Recognizing this is a key to connecting with others more fully and navigating the complexities of human relationships more effectively.

Formal Practices

- Awareness of Breath meditation—twice a day for at least 10 to 15 minutes per session. (Chapter 6, page 58 or http://www.clifsmith.com)
- In the Same Boat meditation—once a day for 7 days. (Chapter 14, page 153 or http://www.clifsmith.com)

Informal Practices

- Choose your own daily activity to do mindfully—every day.
- Catch and Release—Catch and Release one unhelpful internal belief, judgment, or thought each day. (Appendix page 191)
- S.P.A.R.R. practice—during difficult or important conversations. (Appendix page 193)
- S.T.O.P. practice—as needed. (Appendix page 192)
- Gratitude journal—before bed, write down one to three things you are grateful for from the day. What you are grateful for can be big or small.

Signposts

♦ As you practice the In the Same Boat meditation consistently, you may notice a shift in your automatic internal dialogue about other people when they do things that would typically annoy or upset you.

♦ You may surprise yourself by responding more thoughtfully, by being more interested in understanding the person you're talking with, or by invoking S.P.A.R.R. even while in the midst of a highly charged conversation.

♦ You may begin to notice situations in which you've contributed much more to a conflict with someone than you previously thought. Although it might be uncomfortable to realize this, it is not a bad thing. Once you recognize those impulses and behaviors you can begin to Catch and Release them to cease allowing those automatic reactions to unnecessarily negatively affect your life.

Chapter 15

Week 7: Who Watches (Out for) You?

I imagine you have a to-do list. If you do, and it's handy, take a quick look at it. Does it include any entries regarding self-care, taking a break, or exercising? Probably not. I realize we are in week 7 of this program, so you might have an entry for meditation in there now. However, I'd hazard a guess that even exercises from this book are probably not on your to-do list, but rather you have a vague idea that you want to do them and will, when you have time. Isn't it the case, that self-care, exercise, rest, and the like get short shrift in our lives? If self-care even makes it on our to-do list, it's often the lowest priority. It's time for us now to wade into empathy, compassion, and kindness, not just for others but also for ourselves as a type of self-care. The exercises and discussions on these topics aren't mindfulness as much as they are a call to turn toward and strengthen skills we rarely focus on due to the pernicious thought that if we slow down, rest, or lift our foot off the gas pedal for even a moment, we'll "fall behind" or be passed by.

It was Robert Kiyosaki, the famous financial guru, who popularized the phrase, "Pay yourself first" in his wildly successful book, *Rich Dad, Poor Dad*.[1] The "pay yourself first" concept turns conventional wisdom on its head. Conventional wisdom says to pay your bills and some of the money that's left over, if any, can go into savings. The pay yourself first concept says the opposite; divert at least some of your income directly into savings or other assets before paying your bills. It's counterintuitive, but the idea is that you consistently add to your assets, even in very small increments (as low as $25/month, for example), you begin to see compounding growth over the long term. The passive income from your assets begins to become a larger part of your overall income until, one day, the passive income exceeds what you make trading your time for money. The brilliance of the pay yourself first concept is in its simplicity. Consistently apply a small effort, and over time there is a large impact. The same can be done with self-care; we can make small daily investments in taking care of ourselves, which can compound into physical, mental, and emotional well-being, but we often get caught up in our other pursuits and leave self-care on the cutting room floor.

Many of us are already teaching our sons, daughters, nieces, nephews, and neighborhood kids the value of hard work, perseverance, delayed gratification, and sacrifice, as we move through the modern world working toward our goals, dreams, and career aspirations. We converse with other adults at the school bus stop, 4th of July celebrations, Thanksgiving dinners back home, and the cul de sac happy hours; children are right there with us, listening to our conversations. There are ample opportunities for them to witness striving, fighting for, and achieving success and accolades. Important lessons to be learned for sure.

I wonder, dear reader, who watches you and who watches out for you? Who is looking up to you right now, and what are you teaching that person about self-care? This isn't judgment disguised as a question but a sincere inquiry into whether we are taking enough care of ourselves to leave more than a fleeting impression on the minds of the youth around us about the importance of rest and recovery.

The trite but true maxim that we should never sacrifice health for wealth gets shared across social media regularly, but if we are honest, how often have we ever heeded that advice? If we don't heed that advice, what chance do our children have to learn it? Sure, maybe they will eventually come to understand that all elite athletes prioritize rest and recovery in their daily routines, because if they didn't, they wouldn't be elite athletes or able to reach peak performance. What's more likely, though, is that kids are going pick up the behaviors and routines from those closest to them. Do we want our children to work themselves into preventable illness, chronic stress, and burnout, like we so often do? Self-care is not self-*ish*; we cannot hope to take care of those we love or give them a good example to learn from if we don't take care of ourselves.

As I alluded to already, exercises that deliberately cultivate empathy, compassion, and kindness are not mindfulness exercises nor do they cultivate mindfulness. Nonetheless, there is great value in strengthening these skills. Far from being "weak" attributes, these skills, such as turning toward and facing difficulties, strengthen us. They help us connect with and support others, be better leaders, increase our resilience, and enable us to grow the confidence needed to continue pursuing our dreams despite setback and failure.

■ ■ ■

It may seem odd that we are about to focus on empathy, compassion, and kindness when the discussion so far seems to primarily center mostly on self-care. That's a fair reaction. When we hear the terms "empathy," "compassion," and "kindness," we tend to automatically get the sense they are only outward-facing endeavors, things we feel or do for others. However, each of these can be bi-directional. We can express empathy, compassion, and kindness toward ourselves, too, and doing so is a powerful form of self-care. However, it's not necessarily easy to do, especially when some of us bend over backwards to be kind to others while being extremely unkind to ourselves. We will be cultivating these three skills bi-directionally through our exercises, but before we get to them, let's look at each briefly in turn.

Empathy

We'll start with empathy because it's foundational. You cannot have compassion without empathy. The Merriam-Webster online dictionary defines "empathy" as "the action of understanding, being aware of, being sensitive to, and vicariously experiencing the feelings, thoughts, and experience of another of either the past or present without having the feelings, thoughts, and experience fully communicated in an objectively explicit manner."[2] Basically, it means having a sense of what someone else is experiencing without them having to tell you.

We began to deliberately strengthen our capacity for empathy by doing the In the Same Boat meditation in Chapter 14. However, the day you started doing your first mindfulness meditation, you also began strengthening empathy as well, simply as a side effect of the practice. When we start to understand our own inner experience more clearly, we simultaneously begin to learn what others experience as well. As empathy increases, so does our capacity for authentic connection with others regardless of our relationship with them. Of course, no doubt, you've already realized from the In the Same Boat meditation, that it's easier to be empathetic toward someone we know and like than it is toward someone we don't get along with.

Empathy breeds understanding. Just as understanding someone's perspective does not mean we have to agree with it, we also don't have to agree with someone to be empathetic and appreciate where they are coming from or why they hold a specific view. For example, let's look at a controversial political topic: gun control.

Suppose you have two people, Antonio and Samuel, who are on opposite sides of the gun control debate. Samuel grew up in New York City. His experience with guns has always and only been associated with fear, pain, and sadness. His best friend was killed in a mugging when he was 13 years old and a 3-year-old girl was hit and paralyzed by a stray bullet in a drive-by shooting between two rival gangs just a week after his own daughter turned 4 years old. Samuel sees the never-ending stories of murder and other gun violence in his city play out every night on the local news. He's never touched a gun and never wants to be near one. He wants guns off the streets and feels that only trained law enforcement and military personnel should have access to them.

Antonio grew up in rural Texas. His experience with guns has always been associated with enjoyment, responsibility, and connection with loved ones. Antonio had a wonderful relationship with his grandfather, a WWII veteran, who used to take him to the shooting range when he was little. Over the years, Antonio's grandfather continued to take him to the range and on hunting trips when he taught him to treat guns with the utmost respect and to use them responsibly. One of Antonio's most precious memories, and one of the last of his grandfather before he passed away, was when Antonio's grandfather gave him a revolver that had been in their family for three generations. Antonio believes being able to own and use guns is the right of any law-abiding citizen.

The point here isn't about whose position on the issue is the "right" position. The point is that empathy enables us to get a glimpse of what Samuel and Antonio may be experiencing when they get into discussions about this topic. We don't need to agree to understand. If we understand, even a little, where another person is coming from, we are far more likely to have a constructive conversation.

Compassion

If you've ever seen someone in need and had the impulse to help that person, you've experienced compassion. Compassion is empathy in action; it calls on us to take steps to relieve the suffering of another. The impulse to help a senior citizen with a walker get her groceries to her car, reach for your credit card to send funds to help victims of a natural disaster, and pick up books dropped by the new kid on his first day at school are all examples of compassion. We witness some kind of suffering through empathy and then the impulse to act arises, or it doesn't—we don't all have the same baseline level of compassion.

This may not need to be said but I'll say it anyway: self-compassion is compassion directed toward ourselves. Many of us struggle with offering ourselves compassion in response to the challenges, setbacks, and difficult feelings and situations we face. We live in a society that seems to glorify driving ourselves to be at 100% effectiveness even when our bodies or our minds are in serious distress. I'm not talking about the healthy ways in which we push ourselves, such as a having a "wholesome discipline" of self-improvement, exercise, hard work, and so on. I'm talking about the way we often fail to give ourselves compassion in the midst of genuine heartbreak, sadness, regret, or fear.

We have trouble directing compassion toward ourselves. Yet, when we see a friend hurting, we will be compassionate and comforting, not to solve their particular problem but to care for them while they are going through it. We do this with our friends, and parents do it with their children. The father who comforts his daughter who is fighting the flu doesn't believe he's going to cure her; he's supporting and caring for her to help her navigate the challenge. We forget we can be that way toward ourselves. Self-compassion isn't letting ourselves off the hook when we mess up or fail at something; it honors that we are a continuous work in progress and accepts ourselves as we move through life's inevitable ups and downs.

Kindness

Kindness is doing something for someone, whether to relieve suffering, help them out, or just to make them happy, without expecting anything in return. These can be very small to very grand acts, from paying the toll for the driver behind you, to picking up eggs for your neighbor when you go to the grocery store, to anonymously donating computers to a school.

I like to think of kindness sort of like "paying it forward." No one gets through life without receiving some form of kindness from time to time, so offering kindness to others helps me pay forward what has been given to me in the past. One of the best things about kindness is that it not only feels good to the recipient but also it feels good performing the act of kindness itself. Living a life in service to others is one of the surest routes to fulfillment.

Similar to compassion, kindness can be directed toward ourselves. Life is challenging, and as you've probably recognized by now, our inner voice isn't always the nicest companion. Yet, as Allen from week 2 would say, "you've made it this far." Why not try offering some kindness toward yourself in some small and maybe even some large ways? Maybe book a massage or take a day off and indulge in your favorite hobby. Perhaps check in with yourself throughout the day asking, "what do I need right now?" and then stopping and doing it. Allow yourself to close your laptop before you're totally exhausted and get a good night's sleep. Do this in moderation mind you. I don't want to you pull a muscle because you're probably not used to being kind to yourself. Just kidding; have at it, Hoss! Making small investments in self-directed kindness has an outsized impact on your well-being over time.

Cultivating Empathy, Compassion, and Kindness

Empathy, compassion, and kindness do not arise for everyone the same way or in every situation. I'm sure you know some people who are more or less compassionate or kind than others. You may even notice that you are more or less kind or compassionate depending on your mood or whether you've had lunch. similar to any attribute in humans, there is a natural baseline of these traits within all of us, with some people being on the extreme ends of the scale. Whatever your particular baseline, empathy, compassion, and kindness, like mindfulness, can be cultivated through consistent practice. The main practice this week, the Unconditional Friendliness meditation, as well as a new informal practice of performing random acts of kindness, both cultivate these skills.

. . .

This Unconditional Friendliness meditation practice begins to build on the foundation of empathy cultivated by the In the Same Boat meditation and strengthens our capacity for compassion and kindness toward ourselves and others. These can be trained just like any muscle in the body. Additionally, similar to Delving into the Difficult and In the Same Boat, the Unconditional Friendliness meditation is not a mindfulness meditation because we are deliberately bringing up and intensifying certain feelings and emotions.

You can read through the following meditation transcript and then do the exercise on your own without any guidance. However, especially if you are new to this, I recommend doing it as a guided meditation by listening to the audio files noted in the Resources, my teacher account on the Insight Timer app, or at http://www.clifsmith. com; see Appendix page 189 for details. The audio guidance will help you stay on track until you are comfortable and/or interested in doing the exercise on your own.

Unconditional Friendliness Meditation

This meditation practice strengthens our capacity for compassion and kindness toward ourselves and others. These can be trained just like any muscle in the body. Deliberately bringing up feelings of unconditional friendliness and kindness enables us to experience and intensify those feelings, thereby strengthening the related neuropathways in our brain. This enables us to access and "use" these emotions on a more regular basis when interacting with others as well as being more self-compassionate. Treating ourselves as we would a friend helps us release the impulse to harshly attack ourselves. In this meditation, we'll bring up these emotions and offer them to ourselves and others. Let's begin.

♦ Begin by taking a seated posture and settling in for the exercise. Once you're reasonably settled, allow the eyes to close if that's comfortable; otherwise, lower your gaze and soften your focus, tuning into your attention and awareness, just noticing whatever is here in the mind and body for a few moments. Allow whatever you notice to be just as it is and let go of any impulse to wish things to be different or wish them away.

♦ Hold the body with an attitude of unconditional friendliness and care.

♦ Begin to sense the movement of the breath in the heart area, near the center of the chest.

♦ The capacity for unconditional friendliness and kindness exists within all of us. It's the ability to be supportive, open, and kind toward others.

♦ Bring to mind now someone for whom you have deep feelings of affection or love. It can be anyone: a child, friend, partner, or anyone who invokes feelings of love and kindness.

♦ As the image or thought of this person arises, notice any physical response that arises along with it. Perhaps your chest becomes warm, your face softens into a slight smile, or perhaps something else. Then turn toward whatever comes up and invite it in to be fully felt and experienced.

♦ Release this person from the mind and keep on the main stage of awareness the feelings that arose with them.

♦ Now offer these same feelings of unconditional friendliness and kindness to yourself by opening to the following words:

  ♦ May I be safe.
  ♦ May I be healthy.
  ♦ May I have the courage to meet life fully.
  ♦ May I be at peace . . . with the inevitable ups and downs of life.

♦ Notice any feelings that arise and allow them to be just as they are, holding them in mindful awareness.

♦ And now, direct unconditional friendliness and kindness to someone who has supported you in your life. Bring

continued

this person to mind and offer these words silently to them.

- ◆ May you be safe.
- ◆ May you be healthy.
- ◆ May you have the courage to meet life fully.
- ◆ May you be at peace . . . with the inevitable ups and downs of life.

- ◆ Notice any feelings that arise and allow them to be just as they are, holding them in mindful awareness.
- ◆ Bring to mind now someone with whom you may not get along so well, perhaps someone you have friction with from time to time. It's best not to start with the most challenging person but someone who it's not as easy to wish well. See if you can offer these words silently while keeping this person on the main stage of awareness:

- ◆ May you be safe.
- ◆ May you be healthy.
- ◆ May you have the courage to meet life fully.
- ◆ May you be at peace . . . with the inevitable ups and downs of life.

- ◆ Notice any feelings that arise and allow them to be as just as they are, holding the entire experience in nonjudgmental mindful awareness.
- ◆ See if you can open this offer to the wider community, family, friends, neighbors, and colleagues, perhaps expanding to include everyone and yourself as you silently offer these words to all:

- ◆ May we be safe.
- ◆ May we be healthy.
- ◆ May we have the courage to meet life fully.
- ◆ May we be at peace . . . with the inevitable ups and downs of life.

- Notice whatever sensations and feelings arise and sit with them for a few moments.
- Now return attention to the breath for the last few moments of this exercise. Notice the full duration of each inbreath and outbreath.
- I invite you to open your eyes if you've closed them and bring your attention back into the room you're in. Give yourself a moment to get your bearings before moving into the next part of your day.

Common Themes, Challenges, and Questions

Won't giving myself too much self-compassion make me less likely to pursue and reach goals? For example, if I fail and say, "Oh, it's okay; you did your best." Isn't that giving myself an out? Actually no. Studies show that self-compassion increases motivation "to improve personal weaknesses, moral transgressions, and test performance."[3] Self-compassion acknowledges that failure, regret, mistakes, and setbacks are part and parcel of an active engagement with life. Fear is a part of life. Disappointment is a part of life. Loss is a part of life. Doubt is a part of life. All people, across all lands and across all time, have experienced every one of these challenging emotions and situations. You will, too, even if you do not (yet) acknowledge it. Bring some self-compassion to those moments of failure, disappointment, doubt, loss, and regret, and you will be more likely to dust yourself off, learn the lesson that the experience taught you, and continue engaging fully with your life. A wonderful side effect of living in this way is that you will be more equipped to offer compassion to others traversing life's bumpier moments.

Okay, say I buy that empathy, compassion, and kindness are helpful, but c'mon, is it actually useful in the rough-and-tumble corporate world? You were in the military; is compassion helpful there? Absolutely! Who wants to work for or with an unempathetic, heartless, and unkind person? Don't get me wrong, there are people in the corporate world who fit that description exactly. Some have even made it into leadership positions and been able to fly under the radar by saying the right things upwardly and publicly, while being terrible to their people. People only follow them because they have to, not because they want to. Those types of leaders typically get found out by their senior leaders at some point. Compassionate leadership, however, breeds loyalty, dedication, more effective teams, lower stress, and higher job satisfaction. People follow compassionate leaders because they want to, not because they have to.

Key Points, Practices, and Signposts

Key Points

◆ Self-care is not self-*ish*. Whether you are an elite athlete, a top-tier consultant, or in any high-performing role, carving out consistent time for rest and recovery is crucial for peak performance and for being able to take care of your loved ones. Asking yourself, "What do I need right now?" is a great way to explore which of the many forms of self-care are most helpful for you.

◆ Empathy, compassion, and kindness are bi-directional. Offering them to ourselves is also a form of self-care that enhances our ability to grow from the challenges we face in life.

◆ Empathy, compassion, and kindness help us connect more authentically with others. Empathy, in particular, can help us understand others even when we strongly disagree with them. It takes considerable effort to build enough mindfulness to be able to consciously hold different perspectives on the same issue that all happen to be true.

◆ Empathy, compassion, and kindness are skills that can be cultivated through practices designed to evoke and express them.

Formal Practices

◆ Awareness of Breath meditation—twice a day for at least 10 to 15 minutes per session. (Chapter 6, page 58 or http://www.clifsmith.com)

◆ Unconditional Friendliness meditation—once a day for 7 days. (Chapter 15, page 164 or http://www.clifsmith.com)

Informal Practices

- Random acts of kindness—we get better at what we practice, so for the next week do one random act of kindness each day. See Appendix page 193 for ideas.
- Catch and Release—Catch and Release one unhelpful internal belief, judgment, or thought each day. (Appendix page 191)
- S.P.A.R.R. practice—during difficult or important conversations. (Appendix page 193)
- S.T.O.P. practice—as needed. (Appendix page 192)
- Gratitude journal—before bed, write down one to three things you are grateful for from the day. What you are grateful for can be big or small.

Signposts

- As you practice the Unconditional Friendliness meditation consistently, you may find yourself feeling warmth toward others as you move through your day.
- You may also notice that you are able to empathize with people in your social or professional circles even when you are in disagreement with them, which often leads to more productive interactions.
- Consistent practice might lead to a lessening of self-critical inner dialogue and self-attack in reaction to mistakes, failures, or other setbacks.

Chapter 16

Week 8: Maintaining Momentum

Well here we are, week 8. Congratulations! We have covered so much ground in just 8 short weeks together, and I'm so grateful to have been a part of your journey in some small way. You should be very proud to have come this far in service of self-discovery and unlocking exceptional leadership, performance, and well-being. Let's review some of the ground we've covered and discuss ways in which you can maintain the momentum of your practice. Just as your physical health will decline if you stop exercising, a trained mind will begin to atrophy without continued consistent practice.

The insights and effects of a consistent mindfulness practice can be subtle, grow gradually, or nearly knock us off our feet when we realize them. I'm not talking about Enlightenment here. I've already mentioned you can't get that from a book. But, at this point in your practice, you may have experienced some insights into how you show up in the world and how that affects your reality and relationships.

Perhaps you've noticed how quickly the mind retreats into defensive mode in reaction to a story *it* created by guessing at the intent of someone's behavior and then being able to Catch and Release that automatic reaction. Maybe you've become more aware of the tendency of the mind to jump into "doing" mode during any downtime, nearly robbing you of the ability to rest and recover, but you were able to Catch and Release that impulse and take a well-deserved break. You've possibly been the target of harsh criticism for a minor mistake, but instead of reacting, you S.P.A.R.R.ed your way to a productive conversation. Maybe you've begun to see that changing how you respond to the world is often just as good as changing the world.

These are just some of the possible results of your practice; yours may be different. In any case, the journey you are on is your personal journey, there is no "right" pace or place you "should" be by a certain point in time. This is a continuous process of discovery.

■ ■ ■

The terrain we've covered has spanned a number of important topics. Here's a quick recap of the weekly themes:

◆ Week 1: No Trivial Moments: Moving from Autopilot to Aware
◆ Week 2: The Mindset You Bring to Your Experience Matters
◆ Week 3: Do You Have the Story or Does the Story Have You?
◆ Week 4: The Saber-Toothed Tiger of the Modern World: Everything
◆ Week 5: Delving into the Difficult
◆ Week 6: In the Same Boat
◆ Week 7: Who Watches (Out for) You?

In the time spent reading this book and during the home practices, we have discovered how often we are on autopilot, learned how the mindset and attitudes we bring to our experiences affect our reality, and began noticing the stories we tell ourselves and realizing how they can keep us small. We came to see our survival mode jumping into action over non-saber-toothed tiger–related "threats" and turned toward challenging experiences and learned we can let them be and still be okay. We pivoted to the practical and shined a light on our common humanity with others in service to authentic connection and were reminded that self-care and caring for others is just as important as focused effort when it comes to achieving peak performance, individually and collectively.

Now we begin the next step on your continuous journey.

■ ■ ■

The most important thing, when it comes to mindfulness, is to continue to do formal mindfulness meditation practice on a regular, preferably daily, basis. It's quite straightforward. However, when the time spent reading this book and regularly seeing the reminders herein has passed, it may become more difficult. Why? Because, as you are probably acutely aware, incorporating a new behavior into your life is easier said than done, even when you *are* regularly reading a book that's inviting you to practice every day. Plus, this stuff isn't easy!

So, what to do? After you finish the book, go back and reread the introduction to Part II to reconnect with the behavior-building techniques for incorporating a practice into your life, such as preparing your environment, connecting with your intention, and linking the new behavior to a current behavior. Most important, however, just keep doing what you've been learning to do in this book! Let me explain.

When you find that you've "fallen off the wagon" and haven't practiced in a while, which will happen, do exactly what you would do in a formal mindfulness meditation practice when you catch that you are lost in thought. Just begin again, without criticizing yourself for forgetting what you were doing and why you were doing it. When you are doing a Body Scan meditation and get lost in thought, what do you do as soon as you notice it? You just begin again, without criticizing yourself for forgetting what you were doing and why you were doing it.

Missed a day of meditation practice? Missed a week? Missed a month? There is no need to berate yourself or comment about how much time you've wasted. Just begin again, without criticizing yourself for forgetting what you were doing and why you were doing it.

Let's say you forget to meditate 17 days in a row. What might you say to yourself when you realize you've totally forgotten? Perhaps you'd put yourself down and think this meditation thing isn't for you and just quit. What if you missed almost 70 days in a row; would you quit then?

A study from 2012 showed that, when learning to walk, 12- to 19-month old children fall an average of 17 times an *hour*.[1] An hour! One poor kid in the study fell 69 times in 1 hour. And yet the children kept beginning again until they learned to walk. How could they "fail" so much and keep at it? Are they super-special kids? No, they are like most other kids their age; they don't berate themselves constantly every time they "fail," nor do they see their "failure" as a sign of their worthlessness. They lack the language of self-limiting belief, self-attack, and judging whether they are worthy of something. Those unhelpful thought patterns and beliefs haven't been laid down yet, and, therefore, they are not encumbered by them. You don't have to be encumbered by yours, either; that's one of the main points of what we are doing here. We are learning to refrain from getting caught up in and believing every thought and story that bubbles up in our heads.

Failing doesn't mean you're a failure; it means you're learning. Never give up; just begin again—the practice never ends. If you fail to find 20 minutes to practice, find 10 minutes. If you fail to find 10 minutes, find 5 minutes. If you fail to find 5 minutes, find 1 and work your way back up.

A Mindful Day

Before we move into our main practice of this week, I want to leave you with one example of what a mindful day might look like moving forward. A mindful day is one in which you are committed to bringing mindful awareness, as much as you can, into each moment. It does not mean you are or have to be perfect and never get lost in thought. It just means you have the intention of being as present as possible to your life.

A Mindful Day Can Lead to a Mindful Life

◆ Do at least one formal practice, whenever you are most likely to actually do the practice. If that's in the morning, great; do it in the morning. If that's at lunch, great. If that's at night, great. The point is *that* you do it, not when you do it.

◆ Deliberately engage with the present moment throughout your day, and when you notice you've been pulled into a story created by your thinking, use some of the informal practices you've learned to remind yourself that the present moment is where you intended to be. These practices could be the S.T.O.P. practice or even just noticing your breath for a moment. Use transitions in your day as cues to do these exercises, such as when opening/closing your laptop, at the beginning/end of a meeting, after each phone call, when you park your car, and so on. As you begin to string more of these moments together you will be getting closer and closer to bringing seamless attention to all moments of your life.

continued

♦ Delve into the difficult when difficulty arises, if you can. This doesn't mean do the formal Delve into the Difficult meditation each day, but instead just acknowledge those moments when difficulty is present and bring some kindness, (self-)compassion, and openness to them. Ignoring or pushing difficulties away is counterproductive.

♦ Savor pleasurable moments. Similar to Delving into the Difficult, the call here is to turn toward the moment and allow it to be fully felt. It could be a simple as paying very close attention to the first bite of a piece of chocolate or when first stepping into a warm shower. We have many pleasurable moments each day that go by totally unnoticed. We might as well use mindfulness to engage with them, too! Being mindful of pleasurable moments can enhance and amplify the experience. What was a good experience can become great when we bring mindful awareness to the moment.

♦ Deliberately bring your full attention to routine activities such as brushing your teeth, eating, walking, mowing the lawn, gardening, painting, working on your car, doing laundry, and so on. Engage all your senses.

♦ Catch and Release unhelpful limiting beliefs or dialogue when you find you're lost in and buying into them. I mentioned previously in the book that mindfulness isn't about stopping thoughts. A mindful day isn't a day without thoughts. Therefore, because thoughts will still pop up, it's helpful to employ Catch and Release as needed to minimize taking unwise actions or making poor decisions based on the automatic arising of unhelpful internal beliefs, judgments, and thoughts.

♦ Give the gift of attention to everyone with whom you interact. Unless you're a hermit, your life is lived in relationship with others. No one wants to feel like he or she doesn't matter or doesn't matter enough to warrant your full attention. When giving your undivided attention to another person, you are also more likely to be able to invoke the S.P.A.R.R. technique, recognizing that there is a human being in front of you, so you can listen to understand and respond with empathy and compassion.

◆ Remember, the tools you have to navigate the day in a more present and responsive way are always and have always been with you. The breath and body are never in the future nor the past, so you can pay attention to them anytime to bring yourself into the present moment and operate from a place of choice instead of a place of habitual reactivity.

String enough mindful days together, and you'll have lived a mindful life.

The final formal mindfulness meditation exercise we will do in this course is the Just Sitting with Openness meditation. When we do our basic Awareness of Breath meditation, attention is focused very narrowly on the sensations of each in- and outbreath. It's not that other things are not in our awareness, but we are cultivating the skill of concentration in that moment and so are flexing our focus of attention very tightly on the breath. In the Just Sitting with Openness meditation we release that narrow focus and take a much wider per-spective, opening the aperture of our awareness as wide as possible. We can still notice the breath is in the picture, but we are not laser focused on it.

You can read through the following meditation transcript and then do the exercise on your own without any guidance. However, especially if you are new to this, I recommend doing it as a guided meditation by listening to the audio files noted in the Resources, my teacher account on the Insight Timer app, or at http://www.clifsmith. com; see Appendix page 189 for details. The audio guidance will help you stay on track until you are comfortable and/or interested in doing the exercise on your own.

Just Sitting with Openness Meditation

As we begin this meditation, we'll start by focusing in on the breath and then practicing widening the focus of attention and awareness to take in a broader landscape. Let's begin.

◆ Sit up in the chair or whatever is supporting the body and allow both feet to be flat on the floor. Allow the eyes to close, if that feels comfortable, or soften the gaze and angle it down toward the floor. Begin by noticing the sensations of breathing where you feel them most prominently.

◆ You might feel the sensations of air moving in and out of your nose or the sensations associated with the rising and falling of your chest or abdomen as you breathe in and breathe out.

◆ Release any impulse to control the breath. Allow the body to breathe on its own as you pay close attention to the sensations of breathing.

◆ Allow awareness now to expand and encompass the entire body. Notice the full landscape of the body in awareness, including the sensations of breathing, but do not solely focus on them. Merely open to a fuller awareness of what's being experienced in this moment.

◆ The mind and body are still here and, as such, there may be thoughts, feelings, and emotions illuminated by this fuller landscape of awareness. This is perfectly fine.

◆ Notice if there is an edge to awareness and what else is included within it as it continues to expand.

◆ Allow whatever arises in awareness to do so, noticing it while it's there and witnessing it dissipate. Eventually notice the next thing arising in awareness. The call is to merely notice, no pushing away, no pulling in, just allow the process to unfold on its own.

◆ When noticing thoughts or stories that have captivated and captured attention, bring attention back to a narrow focus on the breath, for a few moments before allowing it to expand again, taking in the world that lies within awareness

◆ Just sit in the openness of awareness.

- Where is the mind now? Notice what has captivated the mind without engaging with any automatic judgment that may have arisen along with the noticing. Come back to just sitting in the openness of awareness. No pushing, no pulling, just observing.
- Notice the activity arising in awareness. Sensations arise. Thoughts arise. Perhaps agitation or calmness arise. They can all be here; it's no problem. If any of these captivate and capture the attention, just narrow attention on the breath again for a few moments, before returning to just sitting in the openness of awareness.
- What's being noticed now? Pleasantness arises. Unpleasantness arises. Neutral experience arises. They can all be here; it's no problem. No need to pull them in, nor push them away. Awareness can hold them all within its edgeless landscape.
- Just sit with openness. Allow everything to happen on its own.
- I invite you to open your eyes if you've closed them and bring your attention back into the room you're in. Give yourself a moment to get your bearings before moving into the next part of your day.

Common Themes, Challenges, and Questions

What's the best practice? We've been introduced to so many.
Best is relative. If you are developing concentration, it's tough to find a more effective meditation than Awareness of Breath. It's like sharpening the axe for the open awareness exercises, so doing it regularly is important. You can choose any meditations from the course to do daily but do try to incorporate all of them from time to time because they each have unique yet overlapping impacts on the brain and your ability to be fully present to your experience. You may even consider combining some meditations once you are able to meditate without the guided audio. I call this "choose your own adventure," and as you'll see in the following section it is an option for you moving forward.

In any case, it doesn't matter what label a particular exercise has affixed to it. If you make time for a formal meditation, every day, to practice noticing whatever arises in your awareness, whether thoughts, sensations, or emotions, without grasping at them or pushing them away, and doing so with an attitude of nonjudgmental curiosity and kindness, you are on the right path.

What do you mean the practice never ends? Why do this forever? This isn't actually week 8; it's more like it's the next 8 weeks, 8 months, 8 years, or 8 decades of your life (if you're lucky.) Why continue with this practice this long? Because the horizon of self-discovery continues to move away as you approach it, as surely as the horizon outside your car window does. There's always more to discover because you are always changing. You are a continuous process being changed and shaped by every interaction you have with the world. The person you are right now is not the same as the person you were 5 years ago, 5 months ago, or 5 days ago . . . not even 5 minutes ago. Think about it. You started reading this paragraph about 30 seconds ago and, perhaps for the first time, came across this concept of self-discovery as a horizon you never reach. Not only did that change your brain through neuroplasticity but also it may have changed a particular belief or outlook about self-awareness. Who you are today is constantly slipping away, as who you are becoming begins to appear on the horizon. Just when you think you know exactly who you are, who you are changes. You can't hold on to it or pin it down, just like you can't hold on to a moment as it passes. When we do try to hold on to a past moment or past version of ourselves, it causes us problems and takes us out of fully experiencing life now. Therefore, we continue the practice of watching and learning or perhaps more appropriately, *un*learning who we were so we can be who we are in this moment.

What's the most important thing to know as I continue my mindfulness journey? No matter what, continue doing formal mindfulness meditation practice. If you have questions about what you should do next on your mindfulness journey, practice. If you aren't sure if it's working or not, practice. If you are so busy you can't think straight, practice. Practice, practice, practice.

Key Points, Practices, and Signposts

Key Points

◆ Consistent formal mindfulness meditation practice is the key to reaping and sustaining the benefits of mindfulness. Review the Part II introduction for details on helping incorporate the behavior into your life. Similar to the fact that health and fitness will deteriorate if you stop eating healthy and exercising, the skills developed through mindfulness meditation will atrophy if you stop practicing.

◆ When you fall down, get back up. When you miss a session and remember the next day, the next week, or the next month, just begin again. Use what you've learned in the course, notice that you forgot, begin again, and don't beat yourself up about it or tell yourself a story about it. Just begin again.

◆ Live one mindful day at a time to live a mindful life.

Formal Practices

◆ Just Sitting with Openness meditation—once a day for 7 days. (Chapter 16, page 176 or http://www.clifsmith.com)

◆ After week 8—choose your own adventure—pick any meditation from the course to do daily but do try to incorporate all of them from time to time because they each have unique yet overlapping impacts on the brain and your ability to be fully present to your experience. You may even consider combining some. For example, start with Awareness of Breath, move into the Body Scan, and close with Unconditional Friendliness or Just Sitting with Openness.

Informal Practices

Do these during week 8 and beyond:

◆ Just as you fully focus on your meditation practice, bring mindfulness into as many daily activities as possible—brushing your teeth, gardening, eating, washing dishes, and so on.

continued

◆ Random acts of kindness—continue doing one random act of kindness each day. See Appendix page 193 for ideas.

◆ Catch and Release—Catch and Release one unhelpful internal belief, judgment, or thought each day. (Appendix page 191)

◆ S.P.A.R.R. practice—during difficult or important conversations. (Appendix page 193)

◆ S.T.O.P. practice—as needed. (Appendix page 192)

◆ Gratitude journal—before bed, write down one to three things you are grateful for from the day. What you are grateful for can be big or small.

Signposts

◆ You may begin or have already begun to notice physical benefits of your consistent practice. Perhaps you're sleeping better, have more energy, or are less affected by aches and pains that previously consumed your attention.

◆ As you practice the Just Sitting with Openness meditation, you may get a sense that it's not only thoughts, sensations, and emotions that arise and pass away, but every experience arises and passes away in your awareness.

◆ Continued consistent practice can lead to a recognition that, just like your heart is beating on its own and your thoughts are popping up on their own, pretty much everything is happening on its own. When you have *that* recognition, well, that's when it gets really interesting.

Chapter 17

A Final Word

Congratulations again. It's my sincerest wish that you've come through this experience with new insights into yourself and your engagement with your life, work, and relationships. The thing about self-discovery through mindfulness and the other exercises we've done, is that we quickly realize the barriers between the different aspects of our life are artificial. You may have picked up this book in order to improve your performance, leadership, or well-being while negotiating your professional career but I'm sure that's not all that has been impacted.

All facets of your life intersect within you. Like a spider's web, movement in one area of life reverberates throughout the entire structure. You cannot become more mindful with your colleagues and clients without becoming more mindful with your loved ones. When you learn to respond more wisely to criticism in the workplace, your ability to notice your own reactivity at home also improves. When the muscles of empathy and compassion are strengthened, everyone in your world is the beneficiary.

Our lives aren't discrete compartmented business units, as much as we might like them to be. There is an ever-changing push and pull and we can realize the different parts of our life do not need to be in competition with one another. When we pay close attention, we can begin to notice this ebb and flow and respond to that area of life that needs our attention the most, be it work, family, relationships, or our social contributions. When you do this, you teach others to do this, and that's leadership.

As the reading of this book moves from the present to the past, remember: there are no trivial moments; moments are made trivial by not paying attention to them.

Acknowledgments

We are born into this world helpless, shaking, and scared, and if we are lucky, we are immediately embraced and comforted by our mothers. From that day forward we can never say we made it to where we are in life without the support of others. It's quite similar with writing a book.

As much as writing may feel like a solo endeavor, the words landing on the page are not our words alone. They are words given us by our parents, siblings, friends, colleagues, teachers, newscasters, podcasters, and by authors of any book we've ever read and filtered through our life experiences. So, in a very real sense, everyone I've ever had a conversation with or whose words I've heard or read has helped make this book a reality. If you fall into this general category, I thank you.

As for specific people, there is one person who must be thanked first: my beloved mother. I would not be the man I am today if you were not the selfless, loving, determined, and resourceful mother you are. You taught me to love, to be compassionate, and to not start fights but to finish them if they were started. Any positive traits in me, such as kindness, generosity, integrity, selflessness, resilience, and perseverance, came from you. Thank you, Mom, for all you've done for me and for just being who you are. This book would not exist without you and your support.

Any negative traits I have, such as cursing, drinking, and wanting to spend an inordinate amount of time in the woods around a campfire, probably came from the folks on this next list. To the following men in my life who stepped into the vacuum when I needed guidance as a young man trying to find my way, Howard (deceased), Ernie, Clif (deceased), "Kuhnie" (deceased), Jr., Ray, Rod, and Gary: thanks for giving me good examples of men who worked hard, played hard, and loved, provided for, and protected family above all else. I appreciate all the time and attention you gave me when you didn't have to give any. Of course, none of you could have done any of that without the advice and consent of your lovely wives, so thanks, too, to Colleen (deceased), Lori, Mary, Louise (deceased), Sis,

Jean, Diane, and Annette for letting those jokers help me out and for being amazing, strong, and loving women.

Special thanks to Jen Shaw for believing I could stand in front of a crowd of 3,600 people and deliver a powerful keynote that could change lives. This opportunity changed everything.

Special thanks to Jessica Frankel for encouraging me to share my story on stage when it was the last thing I wanted to do.

Thank you, Bowman Kell and Kelly Dolson, for your trust in me to deliver my first "big" keynotes at EY events. You took a risk, and for that I'm truly grateful.

Thank you, Leonie Schell, for starting the Mindfulness Network at EY; that one pebble you threw into the pond is still making ripples today. Thanks also to Amanda Hart and Josta Kolkman for leading and expanding the reach and content of the network.

Special thanks to Tal Goldhamer for supporting the ambitious idea that "Mindfulness Leader" could be a role at EY and for your support of my efforts to bring these teachings to our colleagues, clients, and others.

Thank you, Steven Hickman, Beth Mulligan, Rich Fernandez, and Meg Levie, for being wonderful mindfulness teachers and true examples of embodiment of the principles we teach.

Thank you, Randall Trani and Eric Maddox, for your friendship, advice, insights, and encouragement throughout this process.

Special thanks to Jason Trost, Kristin Conklin, Keyshia Crawford, and Sammi Soriano for being so generous with your time and talent to help make this book better.

Thanks to Ronaldo Abe, Hava Adziashvili, Scott Askins, Traci Baker-Wilson, Dan Black, Julie Bloom, Anna Bourne, Ken Bouyer, Emily Bray, George Brooks, David Bruesehoff, Nick Burkett-Caudell, Milene Carvalho, Grace Chang, Jake Chun, Ashley Clayton, Juliano Monteiro Costa, Josue Fumero Delgado, Rohan Dewar, Diana Diaz, Gerry Dixon, Paul Donato, Michelle Donovan, Herb Engert, Kathy Farrell-Christoforatos, George Flynn, Judith Freitag, Lauren Galan, Mitchell Gordon, Kathy Grau, Kelly Grier, Susan Haidai, Laura Hanson, Lee Henderson, Michael Herrinton, Maisie Ho, Beth Hopkins, Yulia Ivanova, Kristin Jacob, Rich Jeanneret, Katie Johnston, Kasey Kemp, Rachel Kessler, Tatyana Kovalchuk, Ibi Krukrubo, Hannah Kwak, Eileen Legg, Katie Lei, Traci Lembke, Laura Lenz, Michelle Leung, Jason Levinson, Sherri Libin, Marci Mackay, Jennifer Maddox, Ali Master, Marybeth Matos, Kevin Nagel, Jan Nevidal, Elisa Nieschawer, Oscar Santos Oviedo, Antonella Padova, Mihaela Panait, Deborah Pargmann, Jeannine Pereira, Rita Perivolarys, Chris Phillips, Jen Pratt,

Dawn Quinn, Hasan Rafiq, Marna Ricker, Parminder Sambhi, Rafael Sayagues, Lisa Schiffman, Anthony Sgammato, John Short, Beatrice Sidler, Carolyn Slaski, Amanda Smith, Jeff Stier, Pavel Stika, Arun Subhas, Thear Suzuki, Lauren Taniguchi, Melissa Teruoka, Wendy Tsau, Melissa Ungar, Kevin Virostek, Helen Walsh, Michael Weiner, Katarina Wenk-Bodenmiller, and the more than 70 EY Mindfulness Network Champions around the world.

There are so many who have been supportive of me bringing mindfulness to EY and our clients, who have invited me to speak, made an introduction, shared the impact my keynote or course had on them, or offered to help me in some way; I know I've missed some. Please accept my apology if you're not on this list and should be.

Special thanks to early endorsers of the book, Arianna Huffington, Robert Greene, Doro Bush Koch, Brooke Finlayson, Mark Campbell, Steven Hickman, Representative Michael Waltz, Eric Maddox, and Ed Herbst. I'm honored by your willingness to support my first book and I know your comments will help get this message out to a much broader audience.

Thanks to Mike Campbell at John Wiley & Sons for believing that my story could have a positive impact on others, for your editorial advice, and for your patience while working with "Nick, the new guy" over here. Also, thanks to your very wise fiancée, Haley, for suggesting that you reach out after she saw my keynote.

Thanks to Louise Ducas for your advice and insights. You helped make an opaque process clear.

Thanks to the more than 60,000 people who have attended my keynotes, workshops, and 8-week mindful leadership courses since 2016. The emails, social media posts, and post-talk comments you've shared with me about the impact I've had on you are some of the most fulfilling, uplifting, and heartfelt stories I've ever heard. Please keep sending them and please keep practicing.

Thanks to all my brothers and sisters in the US Army, Department of Defense, and Intelligence Community for your continued commitment to serving our country and preserving our way of life.

Last, but certainly not least, special thanks to Jennifer and Alexander, the loves of my life. More than any, you have had to endure the long days and late nights as I worked to finish this book during the "Summer of COVID-19" while doing my regular full-time job. I'm so grateful for your support, patience, and love. Thank you both from the bottom of my heart; I could never have written this book without you. Let's go on vacation now; you get to pick where.

About the Author

Clif Smith, a US Army veteran, former diplomat, and intelligence officer, serves as Ernst and Young (EY) LLP's Americas Mindfulness Leader and is an internationally recognized leader for bringing mindfulness into the corporate world. Clif brings his story and more than 25 years of experience leading through high-pressure situations into his teachings and demonstrates the value of adopting mindfulness as a fundamental part of our personal and professional lives. Following his passion for developing others, he built EY's Mindful Leadership program, delivering practical training to more than 60,000 people, including EY professionals and clients, with measurable impact on performance, leadership, and well-being.

Before devoting much of his time to creating and managing mindfulness programs, Clif led EY into a new market, winning multimillion-dollar deals for the firm as an account leader in the government and public sector practice. Immediately prior to joining EY, he managed diligence projects across several sectors, including financial services, telecommunications, and government, at private investment firm Granahan McCourt Capital (GMC). Prior to GMC, he was a vice president at JP Morgan Chase, where he helped create the firm's first cyber threat and protective intelligence collection, reporting, and analysis policy and program. Clif's experience in the private sector is preceded by 17 years in the US Department of Defense, Defense Intelligence Agency, and broader Intelligence Community, where he served as an intelligence officer managing and carrying out signals intelligence and clandestine and overt human intelligence collection operations around the globe, including deployments to Afghanistan and Iraq.

Clif's personal journey from poverty to prosperity is a key motivating factor for his work as an executive coach, mindfulness teacher, and keynote speaker helping others achieve success despite their self-limiting beliefs and challenging circumstances. His one-on-one coaching clients have included CEOs and other senior executives, university administrators, veterans, troubled youth, and others. His keynotes, as well as his insights gleaned from successfully bringing mindfulness into the corporate setting, are sought after by many organizations, including major universities, corporations, leadership conferences, and nonprofits nationally and internationally.

Clif is a mindfulness-based stress reduction teacher, a certified Search Inside Yourself Leadership Institute Mindfulness and Emotional Intelligence teacher, an ICF-certified executive coach, and an accomplished public speaker. He has a bachelor of science in business information systems from Bellevue University and master of public administration from Harvard University's John F. Kennedy School of Government.

Clif and his wife, Jen, live with their son in Virginia.

Appendix

Resources

Stay in touch!

Follow me on LinkedIn: https://www.linkedin.com/in/clifsmith/

Follow me on Twitter (@MindfulClif): https://twitter.com/mindfulclif

Follow me on Facebook: https://fb.me/mindfulclif

Guided meditations for the course and other mindfulness resources can be found at the following locations:

www.clifsmith.com

This is the website that contains information regarding my book, mindfulness training, speaking, and executive coaching. You will also find all referenced guided audio tracks labeled in accordance with the meditation titles in the book.

Insight Timer App

The mindfulness exercises outlined in this book can be accessed via this free app by following these directions:

1. Download and install Insight Timer. You will be required to create an account, but you do not need to sign up for any paid subscriptions to use Insight Timer. The app can be downloaded directly from your phone's app store. If you have trouble finding the app, go to www.insighttimer.com for additional instructions for obtaining the app.
2. Once downloaded, launch the app and sign up with an email account. You do not need a premium (members plus) account.
3. Click the search icon and search for "Clif Smith" and you will find my teacher profile.
4. Click the "follow" icon and you will have free access to all the guided meditations for the course in this book.

SoundCloud

SoundCloud is a music and audio platform where I also host guided mindfulness meditation practice audio files. The following web address will take you directly to my profile page, where you will find the meditation audio tracks labeled in accordance with the meditation titles in the book:

https://soundcloud.com/user-662199178

Formal Practice List

The following are the formal practices included in the course, in which week(s) they are the primary practice, and the page numbers where you can find them in this book.

1. Awareness of Breath meditation
   a. Week: Each week
   b. Pages 58
2. Body Scan meditation
   a. Weeks: 1 and 2
   b. Pages 89
3. Sounds, Thoughts, and Emotions meditation
   a. Weeks: 3 and 4
   b. Pages 114
4. Delving into the Difficult meditation
   a. Week: 5
   b. Pages 136
5. In the Same Boat meditation
   a. Week: 6
   b. Pages 153
6. Unconditional Friendliness meditation
   a. Week: 7
   b. Pages 164
7. Just Sitting with Openness meditation
   a. Week: 8
   b. Pages 176

Informal Practice List

4, 3, 2, 1

Take a moment at least once today when you intentionally notice 4 things you see, 3 things you hear, 2 things you feel, and 1 thing you smell.

90-Second Noticing
Take 90 seconds after each meeting/piece of work to focus on your breathing. Really notice the qualities of your breathing. Is it fast? Is it slow? Is it smooth? Is it halted? Don't try to change it, just notice it. At the end of the day reflect on how taking 90 seconds to notice your breathing has affected your day.

Catch and Release
Use the "Catch and Release" technique to notice and let go of unhelpful internal dialogue and fear-driven thinking. When you "Catch" yourself buying into an unhelpful thought, "Release" it and any automatic impulse to believe or follow it. For example, "I'm not good enough." Catch and Release it. "I'll never learn this." Catch and Release it. "If only we were rich, then we'd be happy." Catch and Release it. This one technique alone can massively change your life.

Gratitude Journal
Before bed, write down one to three things you are grateful for from the day. What you are grateful for can be big (got a promotion) or small (had a refreshing glass of water).

Mindful Drinking
Spend some time in the morning or evening drinking a cup of tea or coffee (or another beverage) and give your full attention to the experience of drinking it. Allow yourself to notice the aroma, feel the warmth, experience the flavor washing over your tongue, the sensations of the liquid moving down your throat, and so on. Notice all sensations present when drinking the beverage; if your mind wanders to other things—future, past, and so on—gently escort your attention back to where you intended it to be . . . on experiencing your drink.

Mindful Eating
Eat alone or with friends, silently with no other distractions (no phone, computer, or anything to read). What flavors do you perceive? What is the texture? Hot or cold?

Mindful Listening
In your meetings/conversations with colleagues during the day, try to actively and mindfully listen. Try not to get drawn into judging what your colleague is saying or allowing your mind to get distracted

to thinking about what you want to say in response. When your mind wanders, gently bring it back to the meeting/conversation you are currently involved in. Reflect at the end of the day how mindfully listening affected the quality of the meetings/conversations you had that day.

MINDFUL MEETINGS
Do the S.T.O.P. practice before at least two of your daily meetings and observe any changes in the way you are behaving in those meetings. Are you more productive? Are you more relaxed? Are you less tired at the end of the meeting/day? Are you more flexible and open to other people's ideas and perspectives? Are you more creative and assertive?

MINDFUL SHOWERING
Spend the entire shower noticing how the water feels, the warmth, the coolness when leaving the shower. Notice the sound of the water, your breath, the steam rising. This is in contrast to a typical shower when you might be thinking of your first meeting, a big presentation, regretting something, worrying, and so on.

MINDFUL TOOTHBRUSHING
Be mindful of your arm moving from side to side and the sound of the brush against your teeth. Be mindful of each tooth and the sensation of the brush against your gums.

MINDFUL WALKING
Choose a short distance (walking to the printer, restroom, coffee station) and focus on your feet as you walk, noticing how your foot lands on the floor. What part of your foot lands first? The heel, ball, toes? Give full attention to the act of walking.

S.T.O.P. PRACTICE
    S—Stop. Pause and stop all activity for just a moment or two.
    T—Take a breath. Take a breath and notice the sensations of breathing just like we do in the Awareness of Breath exercise. Perhaps you notice cool air coming in your nose and warm air coming out. Taking a deep breath is optional.
    O—Observe. Notice something in your external environment. Perhaps notice the pattern in the carpet, items on your desk, pictures or paintings on the wall. Then turn that

focus inward and notice what's happening inside you. What thoughts, feelings, and emotions are present? Don't try to push them away or suppress them but instead acknowledge their presence.

P—Pose and Proceed. Pose the question to yourself silently, "What's important now?" Then allow, if you can, what comes up in response to that question to inform your intention for the next moment of your day.

WHAT DO YOU SEE?

Look around and notice five things (using your eyes). What shape, size, color, and texture are these images?

RANDOM ACTS OF KINDNESS IDEAS

- Send flowers for no reason.
- Get coffee for a coworker.
- Allow someone who seems to be in a hurry to go in front of you in line.
- Assist a neighbor in carrying his or her shopping.
- Send a note to your boss giving kudos to someone else on the team.
- Tell a coworker how much you appreciate his or her hard work.
- Do something for your partner or roommate you know he or she hates doing.
- Share your umbrella with someone caught in the rain.
- Donate some items you no longer need.
- Let a friend or family member know how much you appreciate him or her.
- Put together a welcome basket for a new neighbor.
- Allow someone to merge into your lane even if that person didn't wait on the long exit ramp.
- Give the gift of your full attention to someone.
- Send school supplies to a local elementary school.
- Offer to do grocery store trips for an elderly neighbor.

S.P.A.R.R. TECHNIQUE

S—Stop as soon as you catch that a comment has triggered an automatic reaction within you or **Stop** in response to a comment or question in another context that may be important to you so you can respond thoughtfully.

P—Pause for a moment to gather yourself and complete the next steps.

A—Assess what emotions and thoughts you are aware of in yourself and that may be in the person you're talking with during the interaction, and assess what a wiser course of action might be, as opposed to going with your automatic reaction. You may want to confirm the other person's emotions and thoughts during the response step if appropriate, because, as we've seen, our interpretations can be wildly inaccurate. Part of inquiring about thoughts and emotions without judgment is to acknowledge them in the other person. This requires that you pay attention and listen during the interaction.

R—Recognize there is a human being on the other end of the communication and acknowledge, accept, and be open to that person's situation, agenda, and point of view. This doesn't mean you have to agree with that person; it's more about trying to understand and exercising empathy. If you keep your own agenda as the primary motivation for the interaction, you will miss out on information the person is sending, and you won't build trust because the person will know that you are more interested in what you want than you are in understanding him or her.

R—Respond deliberately and in a way that supports effective communication.

Notes

Introduction

1. https://www.dimensions.guide/element/track-and-field-400m-running-track
2. Hróbjartsson, A., & Norup, M. (2003). The use of placebo interventions in medical practice—A national questionnaire survey of Danish clinicians. *Evaluation & the Health Professions, 26*(2), 153–165. https://doi.org/10.1177/0163278703026002002
3. Luthar, S., Small, P., & Ciciolla, L. (2018). Adolescents from upper middle class communities: Substance misuse and addiction across early adulthood. *Development and Psychopathology, 30*(1), 315–335. https://doi.org/10.1017/S0954579417000645

Chapter 1

1. https://www.toysfortots.org
2. https://www.sotkd.us
3. Eric Maddox—you may have heard of him; he did all the interrogations that uncovered the whereabouts and led to the capture of Saddam Hussein. Read his book, *Capturing Saddam: The Hunt for Saddam Hussein—As Told by the Unlikely Interrogator Who Spearheaded the Mission*. He is also an amazing speaker for corporate and other events when inspiring the audience is a high priority. Invite him to speak by connecting with him at www.ericmaddox.com.
4. https://www.mpc.edu
5. https://www.bellevue.edu/

Chapter 2

1. https://www.marketsandmarkets.com/Market-Reports/digital-transformation-market-43010479.html
2. Anthony, S. D., Viguerie, S. P., & Waldeck, A. (2016, Spring). Corporate longevity: Turbulence ahead for large organizations. Executive Briefing. https://www.innosight.com/wp-content/uploads/2016/08/Corporate-Longevity-2016-Final.pdf
3. Davenport, T. H., & Beck, J. C. (2005). *The attention economy: Understanding the new currency of business*. Harvard Business School.

4. Aamoth, D. (2014, August 18). First smartphone turns 20: Fun facts about Simon. *Time*. https://time.com/3137005/first-smartphone-ibm-simon/

5. Ibid.

6. How BlackBerry conquered the world (2005, March 23). *CNN*. https://www.cnn.com/2005/BUSINESS/03/23/blackberry.rim/

7. Ibid.

8. Marques, R.P.F., & Lopes Batista, J. C. (2017). *Information and communication overload in the digital age* (p. 28). Information Science Reference.

9. The Radicati Group, Inc. (n.d.). Email statistics report, 2015–2019. https://www.radicati.com/wp/wp-content/uploads/2015/02/Email-Statistics-Report-2015-2019-Executive-Summary.pdf

10. He, A. (2019, May 31). Average time spent with media in 2019 has plateaued. EMarketer. https://www.emarketer.com/content/us-time-spent-with-media-in-2019-has-plateaued-with-digital-making-up-losses-by-old-media

11. https://www.ics.uci.edu/~gmark/Home_page/Welcome.html

12. Schachter, H. (2014, August 28). Stressed and cranky? E-mail could be the cause. *The Globe and Mail*. https://www.theglobeandmail.com/report-on-business/careers/career-advice/life-at-work/stressed-and-cranky-e-mail-could-be-the-cause/article20208337

13. Monsell, S. (2003). Task switching. *Trends in Cognitive Sciences, 7*(3), 134–140. https://doi.org/10.1016/S1364-6613(03)00028-7

14. Gonzalez, V., & Mark, G. (2004). Constant, constant, multi-tasking craziness: Managing multiple working spheres. *Proceedings of ACM CHI'04*, 113–120; Mark, G., Gonzalez, V. M., & Harris, J. (2005). No task left behind? Examining the nature of fragmented work. *Proceeding of the SIGCHI Conference on Human Factors in Computing Systems* (pp. 321–330). ACM Press.

15. American Psychological Association. (2017, February 23). APA's survey finds constantly checking electronic devices linked to significant stress for most Americans. https://www.apa.org/news/press/releases/2017/02/checking-devices

16. Killingsworth, M. A., & Gilbert, D. T. (2010). A wandering mind is an unhappy mind. *Science, 330*(6006), 932. https://doi.org/10.1126/science.1192439

17. Ibid.

18. The Forum is the main student gathering place at the John F. Kennedy School of Government at Harvard University and is where the school routinely hosts world leaders, philanthropists, politicians, and other public servants to have robust discussions with the faculty and student body.

19. C. K., L. (2011, January 9). Louis C.K. - The miracle of flight. Comedy Central. http://www.cc.com/video-clips/1myllo/the-miracle-of-flight

20. Unruh Jr., J. D. (1975). *The plains across the overland: Emigrants and the trans-Mississippi west, 1840–1860*. University of Illinois Press.
21. McNeese, T. (2009). *The Donner party: A doomed journey*. Chelsea House.

Chapter 3

1. P-hacking is a method unscrupulous researchers use to manipulate their findings by cherry-picking data to ensure a statistically significant result is "discovered."
2. Lazar, S. W., Kerr, C. E., Wasserman, R. H., Gray, J. R., Greve, D. N., Treadway, M. T., McGarvey, M., Quinn, B. T., Dusek, J. A., Benson, H., Rauch, S. L., Moore, C. I., & Fischl, B. (2005). Meditation experience is associated with increased cortical thickness. *Neuroreport, 16*(7), 1893–1897. https://doi.org/10.1097/01.wnr.0000186598.66243.19
3. Taren, A. A., Creswell, J. D., & Gianaros, P. J. (2013). Dispositional mindfulness co-varies with smaller amygdala and caudate volumes in community adults. *PLoS ONE, 8*(5), e64574. https://doi.org/10.1371/journal.pone.0064574
4. Hölzel, B. K., Ott, U., Hempel, H., Hackl, A., Wolf, K., Stark, R., & Vaitl, D. (2007). Differential engagement of anterior cingulate and adjacent medial frontal cortex in adept meditators and non-meditators. *Neuroscience Letters, 421*(1), 16–21.
5. Hölzel, B. K., Carmody, J., Vangel, M., Congleton, C., Yerramsetti, S. M., Gard, T., & Lazar, S. W. (2011). Mindfulness practice leads to increases in regional brain gray matter density. *Psychiatry Research, 191*(1), 36–43. https://doi.org/10.1016/j.pscychresns.2010.08.006; Luders, E., Toga, A. W., Lepore, N., & Gaser, C. (2009). The underlying anatomical correlates of long-term meditation: Larger hippocampal and frontal volumes of gray matter. *Neuroimage, 45*(3), 672–678. https://doi.org/10.1016/j.neuroimage.2008.12.061; Greenberg, J., Romero, V. I., Elkin-Frankston, S., Bezdek, M. A., Schumacher, E. H., & Lazar, S. W. (2019). Reduced interference in working memory following mindfulness training is associated with increases in hippocampal volume. *Brain Imaging and Behavior, 13*(2), 366–376. https://doi.org/10.1007/s11682-018-9858-4
6. Jha, A. P., Stanley, E. A., Kiyonaga, A., Wong, L., & Gelfand, L. (2010). Examining the protective effects of mindfulness training on working memory capacity and affective experience. *Emotion, 10*(1), 54–64. https://doi.org/10.1037/a0018438
7. Mrazek, M. D., Franklin, M. S., Tarchin Phillips, D., Baird, B., & Schooler, J. W. (2013). Mindfulness training improves working memory capacity and GRE performance while reducing mind wandering. *Psychological Science, 24*(5), 776–781. https://doi.org/10.1177/0956797612459659

8. Hölzel, B. K., Ott, U., Gard, T., Hempel, H., Weygandt, M., Morgen, K., & Vaitl, D. (2008). Investigation of mindfulness meditation practitioners with voxel-based morphometry. *Social Cognitive and Affective Neuroscience, 3*(1), 55–61. https://doi.org/10.1093/scan/nsm038

9. Laneri, D., Krach, S., Paulus, F. M., Kanske, P., Schuster, V., Sommer, J., & Müller-Pinzler, L. (2017). Mindfulness meditation regulates anterior insula activity during empathy for social pain. *Human Brain Mapping, 38*(8), 4034–4046. https://doi.org/10.1002/hbm.23646

10. Resources. (2020, February 13). American Mindfulness Research Association. https://goamra.org/resources/

11. Goleman, D., & Davidson, R. J. (2018). *Altered traits: Science reveals how meditation changes your mind, brain, and body.* Avery; Hanson, R., & Mendius, R. (2009). *Buddha's brain: The practical neuroscience of happiness, love, and wisdom.* New Harbinger Publications.

Chapter 4

1. Goldstein, E. (2013). *The now effect: How this moment can change the rest of your life.* Atria Paperback.

Chapter 5

1. Search performed on April 2, 2020.
2. https://billmoyers.com/series/healing-and-the-mind/
3. Kabat-Zinn, J. (2004). *Wherever you go, there you are* (p. 4). Piatkus.
4. Holiday, R. (2019). *Stillness is the key: An ancient strategy for modern life.* Profile Books.

Chapter 7

1. My comments here about the point of dancing and the symphony are inspired by comments I've heard in recordings of Alan Watts giving talks. Watts made a number of comments that the point of dancing is not to get to certain spots on the dance floor nor is the point of a symphony to get to the end of the symphony, but I could not locate any specific works where I could accurately cite his exact phrasing.

Chapter 8

1. Fogg, B. J. (2020). *Tiny habits: + the small changes that change everything.* Houghton Mifflin Harcourt; Clear, J. (2018). *Atomic habits: An easy & proven way to build good habits & break bad ones.* Avery.

Chapter 10

1. Kabat-Zinn, J. (2013). *Full catastrophe living: Using the wisdom of your body and mind to face stress, pain, and illness* (pp. 19–38). Bantam Books.
2. Williams, J.M.G., Penman, D., & Kabat-Zinn, J. (2012). *Mindfulness: An eight-week plan for finding peace in a frantic world* (pp. 28–45). Rodale Books.
3. Centers for Disease Control and Prevention. (2017). CDC - Data and Statistics - Sleep and Sleep Disorders. https://www.cdc.gov/sleep/data_statistics.html

Chapter 11

1. The Sounds, Thoughts, and Emotions meditation is adapted from the Sounds and Thoughts meditation in Williams, J.M.G., Penman, D., & Kabat-Zinn, J. (2012). *Mindfulness: An eight-week plan for finding peace in a frantic world* (pp. 143–147). Rodale Books.

Chapter 12

1. Salleh, M. R. (2008). Life event, stress and illness. *The Malaysian Journal of Medical Sciences, 15*(4), 9–18.

Chapter 13

1. Taleb, N. N. (2016). *Antifragile: Things that gain from disorder.* Random House.
2. Rick Hanson, PhD, has written extensively on the differences between reactions versus responses, and although I'm not quoting him specifically, undoubtably his work has influenced my writing here. For a deeper dive into the differences between reactions and responses check out his books *Resilient: How to Grow an Unshakable Core of Calm, Strength, and Happiness* and *Just One Thing: Developing a Buddha Brain One Simple Practice at a Time.*
3. Delving into the Difficult is adapted from the Exploring Difficulties meditation described in Williams, J.M.G., Penman, D., & Kabat-Zinn, J. (2012). *Mindfulness: An eight-week plan for finding peace in a frantic world* (pp. 172–174). Rodale Books.

Chapter 14

1. Stone, D., Heen, S., & Patton, P. (2010). *Difficult conversations: How to discuss what matters most.* Penguin Books. This story, and part of the

approach to analyzing and understanding it, is inspired by this wonderful book. Buy it, read it, then read it again.

2. I adapted this practice from a similar one I learned in an intelligence collection training course and have not been able to attribute it to any publication or purpose. It is not a classified technique.

3. In the Same Boat meditation is an adaptation of the Just Like Me meditation from Tan, C.-M. (2012). *Search inside yourself: The unexpected path to achieving success, happiness (and world peace)*. Harper One.

Chapter 15

1. Kiyosaki, R. T., & Lechter, S. L. (1998). *Rich dad, poor dad: What the rich teach their kids about money that the poor and middle class do not!* TechPress.

2. Empathy. (n.d.). Merriam-Webster. https://www.merriam-webster.com/dictionary/empathy

3. Breines, J. G., & Chen, S. (2012). Self-compassion increases self-improvement motivation. *Personality and Social Psychology Bulletin*, *38*(9), 1133–1143. https://doi.org/10.1177/0146167212445599

Chapter 16

1. Adolph, K. E., Cole, W. G., Komati, M., Garciaguirre, J. S., Badaly, D., Lingeman, J. M., Chan, G.L.Y., & Sotsky, R. B. (2012). How do you learn to walk? Thousands of steps and dozens of falls per day. *Psychological Science, 23*(11), 1387–1394. https://doi.org/10.1177/0956797612446346

Index

NOTE: Page references in *italics* refer to figures.